THE FLAWS THAT KILL OUR DEMOCRACY

AF499381

THE FLAWS THAT KILL OUR DEMOCRACY

—— • ——

VERSION 1.0

KLAAS MENSAERT

2020

Cover Illustration: The illustration depicts the Statue of Liberty—a symbol of our democracy—composed of a network of people. However, because of the exclusive party system, a gap is created between people of different parties and therefore within our democracy.

© Klaas Mensaert 2020
Some rights reserved. No part of this publication may be reproduced, stored in a retrieval system, or transmitted in any form or by any means—electronic, mechanical, or via photocopying, recording, or otherwise—for commercial purposes without the prior permission of the author. This work is licensed under a Creative Commons Attribution-NonCommercial-NoDerivatives 4.0 International License.

This book was written by Klaas Mensaert. The opinions expressed in this book are the author's own and do not reflect the view of any of his employers.

Edited by Amanda Koenig (Koenig Editing).
Proofread by Paul Meyer (Meyer Editorial Services).
Book design assistance by Steven Theunis (Armée de Verre).

Contact: klaas@klaasmensaert.be
Website: www.klaasmensaert.be

ISBN: 978-94-6396-570-5
eISBN: 978-94-6396-571-2

CONTENTS

PREFACE

There are some rotten things in our systems of democracy. What many considered to be the best political system is still capable of creating some of the worst policies and most terrible dictators—situations it should prevent.

In this book, I explore some problems and potential solutions for "vanilla representative democracy," as it is implemented in many of our states. Vanilla representative democracy includes the political party system, elections, and parliament. My ideas are not an attempt to generate a closed or final solution; rather, they should inspire discussion and new ideas about representative democracy. This book is a philosophical and scientific work, in the sense that it will pose falsifiable hypotheses.

The book is divided into three chapters, beginning with abstract general notions of decentralization and democracy and their relationship with the economy. Second, I discuss two different forms of political parties and their alleged characteristics. I end with a description of a new parliament and its elections that might satisfy the conditions for the political evolution described in Chapters 1 (Decentralization) and 2 (Exclusive Parties). Although this book reads linearly, neither the thinking nor the writing were linear. In fact, the thought that sparked this book was *contra voting* (giving negative votes to someone), an idea described in Chapter 3 (Representation). Tinkering with this idea and its potential benefits drew me to other ideas, which led me to write this book. I hope some of my thoughts will inspire readers and perhaps generate some benefits for citizens.

This book favors neither the left nor the right, conservatives nor progressives. But it does favor bottom-up vs. top-down, economic entrepreneurs vs. CEOs, social entrepreneurs vs. party bosses, and the people vs. the elite.

ACKNOWLEDGEMENTS

Writing is mostly a solitary dedication. Yet, without a few other people, this work would not have been realized.

I would first like to thank my editor, Amanda Tindall, for making my ideas more structured and understandable. I would also like to thank my proofreader, Paul Meyer, for polishing the manuscript. Many thanks to Steven Theunis, who helped produce an awesome front cover and a beautiful book design. Each of these people loves their craft and supported me in my quest to self-publish this book.

I am very grateful to those who read and gave substantial comments to a premature manuscript. Thank you Stijn Van Hoey, Alexander Borghgraef, and Jolien Goossens. Their enthusiasm, and that of Jan Blommaert, to whom I presented my ideas in 2015, helped me convince myself that these concepts were definitely worth writing down. I would also like to thank the (former) Pirates in Crew Gent, Belgium, and some international members, for my time in that party. My lack of belief is in the current political system—definitely not the people who populate it.

I would also like to thank three people who have been majorly influential in the writing of this book: Moisey Ostrogorski, Karl Popper, and Nassim Taleb. Ostrogorski was a revelation to me—someone with such similar ideas to mine, who had passed away almost one hundred years ago and has been undervalued since. Karl Popper and Nassim Taleb have been hugely important, not just in what I think, but in how I think about problems.

Lastly, I want to thank my friends and family, who kept asking about the book, its ideas, and when it was going to be published. They have been very supportive. A special mention goes to my sister, who helped me with the writing of a synopsis.

PART I

THE FLAWS THAT KILL OUR DEMOCRACY

CHAPTER 1

DECENTRALIZATION

1 MY POLITICAL AWAKENING

Until I went to university, I naively wished that I could become an enlightened, absolute world ruler. I knew that there were many problems in the world and that someone has to fix them. Of course, many people lack good intentions, so it is difficult to find a leader fit for this task. I knew my own good intentions; therefore, I would be the best and most benevolent ruler of the Earth.

Since I have always been very interested in science, and later in philosophy, I stumbled upon the works of Karl Popper. His works taught me that it is the scientific method that enabled us to generate knowledge since the Renaissance (as opposed to a sudden increase in the number of geniuses or of people very driven to find the truth). The scientific method can be regarded as a *bottom-up* process in which people initially generate many hypotheses. Then the better hypotheses are identified and selected based on agreement with reality, usually by experiments and observations. This process of selection is conducted by both the person that suggested the hypothesis and by others. The selection of the best hypothesis begins with reasoning and thought experiments, and it ideally progresses to successfully conducting real experiments that try to falsify the theory.[1] It is this bottom-up process that allows many participants to both suggest and scrutinize new hypotheses and that guarantees the progress of science.

Karl Popper's ideas about political institutions can likewise be considered bottom-up, as he favors piecemeal social engineering over utopian social engineering.[2] In piecemeal social engineering, one identifies a flaw within the current society and attempts to fix it. After this, the solution is re-evaluated in order to improve society; this process is repeated step-by-step for each flaw. In contrast, utopian social engineering begins with experts who aim to construct a new, ideal society. After these experts generate their blueprint for society, they execute their plan without any further input. Therefore, utopian social engineering does not seek citizen input or criticism because it will only hinder the execution of the blueprint, while piecemeal social engineering depends on criticism to attempt to fix newly identified flaws. Popper's writings convinced me that my wish to be a benevolent ruler was not wise, because society is too complex for any blueprint to succeed. Instead, I should strive for piecemeal social engineering, a bottom-up process, determined by citizens, that can improve the world.

After considering Popper's writings I began reading the works of Nassim Nicholas Taleb. Taleb describes how most changes in our complex society have non-linear effects. For example, the bankruptcy of a billion-dollar company has a much larger effect than the bankruptcies of one hundred companies each worth ten million dollars. So when a system is going to be adjusted, many small changes are better

1 Popper, 1959.
2 Popper, 1945.

than a few big ones. The system can then adjust or react to each small change. This confirms why piecemeal social engineering beats utopian social engineering.

Piecemeal engineering has a dual role in this book. First, I will discuss the best political system currently in use, representative democracy, and I will propose changes to fix its flaws. Piecemeal engineering is therefore applied as a method to the current system. Second, whether a new political system favors piecemeal engineering over utopian engineering will also be important in the evaluation of this new system. Although I mentioned that criticism by citizens is crucial for democracy to function, there is a more general way to describe systems that need variability.

2 (ANTI-)FRAGILITY

Taleb's second relevant idea to this discussion is *anti-fragility*.[3] Generally, fragile things are harmed by variation while resilient things are minimally affected. Taleb, however, notes that variability can be beneficial for some things; he describes this as anti-fragility. Anti-fragile systems benefit from variation as they adapt to and compensate for frequent, small mistakes. In contrast, because fragile systems are harmed by variation, stakeholders of these systems will attempt to control or suppress change. Unable to adapt to information from the suppressed variations, the system will eventually produce an unlikely event with such a large impact that it breaks the system. These are called Black Swan events.

3 Taleb, 2012.

In complex systems, there is an inverse relationship between the fragility of subunits and the fragility of the system. The subunits of a system must be fragile, relative to the system, to make the system anti-fragile. An example with banks and organisms clearly illustrates this principle. Banks must be individually fragile in order to create an anti-fragile banking system. If this is not the case (for example, if banks are too big to fail), then the system will become more susceptible to damage by individual components (banks) caused by variation. Generally, companies must be fragile in order to ensure that an economy is anti-fragile.

This principle can also be observed at multiple hierarchical layers. For example, an organism can be anti-fragile because its cells are fragile. When cells exhibit signals of heavy stress or infection, they are programmed to self-destruct, protecting the organism from complete failure. But the cell can also be anti-fragile, relative to its fragile components (organelles and molecules). When misfolded proteins are detected, they are recycled by the cell. When this hierarchical interplay between fragility and anti-fragility is not present, the system fails. This is why prions (molecules that induce proteins to fold abnormally) can progressively kill cells if not removed. Similarly, cancerous cells, which suppress the cell's ability to self-destruct, can be fatal to an organism.

These concepts are important because the political systems of most democracies seem to be fragile. This overall fragility might be caused by the reduced fragility of the subunits: the political parties. This thesis is supported by two observations.

First, if a subunit of an anti-fragile system performs poorly, it can be removed from the pool. For example, bad restaurants will eventually close and new ones will open. But in politics, this rarely seems to be the case. The same parties promote candidates in election after election. In the United States, Democrats and Republicans (the two ruling parties) alternatively take power—why do these parties not vanish after poor choices decrease their popularity?

Second, as the subunits become less fragile relative to the system, the rules of the subunit become more and more important for the success of the system. In contrast, if the subunits are fragile, then they can be considered as black boxes, because there is no need to micromanage the internal workings of the subunits from the system's standpoint. Then favorable outcomes can be selected from other subunits that do work well. In the United States, the fairness and general workings of the two ruling parties (i.e., organizing and conducting primary elections) are far more important for the success of the political system as a whole than is ideal. In most countries, political parties can choose their own system by which they elect their candidates. This should be reasonable, since political parties are private organizations. Given that there are sufficient candidates presented by the different parties, this process does not pose any danger to the state when some parties fail to select a good candidate. However, in the United States, only one candidate with a reasonable chance of winning is selected by each of the two major parties. A bad selection in the primaries can, therefore, have major implications on who will win in the general election. Therefore, it becomes very important for the primaries to be well regulated. The United States controls this with laws that regulate primaries; these laws are less common in other countries.

Attempting to use naive electoral interventions to stabilize the political landscape might actually make the political system more fragile (because these interventions reduce the fragility of the ruling parties). For example, electoral thresholds make it easier for ruling parties to retain power by limiting or preventing representation if the threshold is not exceeded by contestants during an election. These parties can then achieve supermajorities and change constitutions, actions that may chip away at democracy in a society.

An example of a country in which democracy appears to be deteriorating is Turkey, which has a 10 percent threshold for any party to enter parliament. Plurality systems (in contrast to proportional representation) also seem to reduce the number of parties, making them more anti-fragile. However, at the same time, people's representatives become less dependent on parties, which again makes parties more fragile. These interventions are naive, because, while they propose to increase stability, they only create short-term stability by eliminating variability. However, by making those parties anti-fragile, they increase the risk of long-term instability (by Black Swans), because when the dominating party fails, the whole political system can fail.

Black Swans are the third major concept described by Taleb; they are essential to this work.[4] Black Swans are unpredictable events with large consequences. The consequences can be negative—for example, World War I, World War II, or the September 11th attacks in the United States. They can also be positive though; consider inventions like the internet or the laser. Because they are

4 Taleb, 2007.

inherently unpredictable, we cannot defend against them with knowledge-intensive methods (e.g., models & prediction). Instead, we should design our systems so they are robust to negative Black Swans. Furthermore, when the system is failing, stakeholders should know this as soon as possible so that errors cannot grow. Anti-fragile systems will be less susceptible toward Black Swans because their sub-units will fail individually, providing information about the problem to the entire system.

3 DECENTRALIZATION

Humans have been able to sustain larger communities since they began living more sedentary lifestyles. With advances in technology, we have constructed larger organizations that increase the power of our leaders. While this has led to beneficial endeavors, like building large irrigation systems, it has also contributed to larger man-made catastrophes such as pollution, wars and genocides. While the power of pre-modern societies was restricted by a lack of technology, this eventually gave way to new advances, including fast communication, nuclear capabilities, and advances in hygiene that led to even larger populations. For example, although the Roman Empire was vast, the emperor's power in provinces was limited, partially because communication was very slow, especially compared to today's standards. In contrast, the power of nations in World War I was significantly increased due to a vast train network, wired communication, and other technological advances. This power led to the immense material and human destruction of that war.

So while power seems to be more and more centralized, certain mechanics have been successfully used to limit the centralization of power and, therefore, the risk of large failures. We decentralize our society by making different sources of power independent from one another. One of the simplest ways to decentralize power is geographic separation. Solving problems at the lowest level can ensure that power is limited at higher levels. This principle is known as the subsidiary principle; it was first coined by the Catholic Church, and it should be a cornerstone of the European Union (EU).[5] Another physical separation of power can be seen in time: officials are elected for fixed terms, limiting their accumulated power over time.

Space and time are physical dimensions, so they are very robust in decentralizing power. By creating borders between regions or defining limited political terms, power is distinctly subdivided. However, at a certain point in history, further decentralization was required, and new decentralizations formed along some sociological dimensions. Although they are less concrete, they are employed to separate power much more often. The best known example is the separation of executive, legislative, and judicial power. Other well-known examples are the separation of state and religion (secularism) and the separation of politics and economy (e.g., anti-corruption).

Further subdivisions can also be made within these domains. For example, the Glass–Steagall act separated commercial and investment banks in the United States between

5 Note that nationalistic parties often use the subsidiary principle against the EU. However, they do this inconsistently. They might support the decentralization of a supernational power while supporting centralization of national power.

1933 and 1999. The abolition of the Glass–Steagall act during the presidency of Bill Clinton is regarded by some as a determining factor that lead to the 2008 financial crisis.[6] Leaders that acquire power in multiple domains can more easily become tyrants. Kim Jong-un is a current example of a leader who is not just the head of state; he is also the economic, political, military, and even religious leader of North Korea.

Perhaps the most fundamental guarantees to decentralized power are the rights of the individual. These include freedom of speech, right to a trial before conviction, and property rights, among others. Centralized powers want to execute their plans, and individual rights can be a strong safeguard, protecting society from organized collective stupidity. Individual rights prevent centralized powers from suppressing individual choices, thereby maintaining diversity in society. Diversity is necessary because it includes different social options; similarly, genetic diversity provides options for organisms to react to environmental challenges. In addition to the benefits to society, these freedoms are also profitable to individual citizens themselves. For example, Amartya Sen has illustrated how poverty can be explained as a deficit of freedom.[7]

4 ECONOMY AND POLITICS

Activities such as religion, economics, politics, and justice have been separated in many civilizations. This has proven to be a positive development, because an individ-

6 en.wikipedia.org/wiki/Glass_Steagall_legislation#Aftermath_of_repeal

7 Sen, 1999.

ual's power in one activity is contained and therefore totalitarianism is less likely to develop. However, we should remember that these artificially created domains cannot be fully evaluated in isolation from one another, and each of these activities influences the workings of the others.

The relationship between the economy and politics requires further discussion. First, both the economic and political landscapes are composed of units that are larger than individuals: organizations. Analogies between economic and political organizations might, therefore, provide a better understanding of the potential flaws in our democratic system. Second, although the separation of economic and political power in society has been attempted—for example, by making corruption illegal—the interactions between these realms are still very significant.

Capitalism is both praised and criticized in Western society. According to Wikipedia,[8] capitalism is an economic system in which both the means of production and their operation for profit are privately controlled. I think capitalism works well as an economical system because it reduces overall economic system risks by separating the total economy into smaller entities—private enterprises—thereby allowing them to fail individually. This makes a capitalistic economy anti-fragile; as most entities fail, others can learn from their mistakes. This works by allowing enterprises to obtain private profit (after taxes) as an incentive to take individual risks. This can be contrasted with top-down planned economies (e.g., communism) in which an elite group determines the economic risks that society takes, generally resulting in system-breaking errors and overall fragility.

8 en.wikipedia.org/wiki/Capitalism, on 22/09/2017

The most important message of Adams Smith's *The Wealth of Nations* should not be found in the motivation of the individual—that is, egoism—but in individual decisions, which combine to give a global, positive outcome for many individuals.[9] Because individual problems are most familiar to that individual, each person is best able to solve them, when given the freedom to do so. It is not the merit of egoism that makes capitalism work, but the decentralized mechanisms, regardless of intentions (egoistic or altruistic). The same effects can be observed in political activism, which is often caused by discontent because of local problems (e.g., pollution, civil rights violations, or corruption). Similarly, the sum of all local activism efforts should give us the best outcome for global improvement. Democracy should work regardless of whether the motivations of citizens are selfish or selfless.

Similar to other individual rights, the ability to decentralize capital (and therefore economic power) to the individual should reduce systemic risk. People profit from a business because they take a personal risk. When they fail, others (society) can learn from their mistakes, thereby improving the system. The capitalistic economy has been very successful in making scarce goods/services more available. However, because of its success, there seems to be a notion that capitalism can solve (almost) all problems—as long as we can economize them. That is to say, if we reformulate a challenge into a scarcity problem, then we can tackle it with capitalism. This is something I am totally against!

By way of analogy, how effective is a saw when cooking a stew? Saws will never be useful for cooking meals. Like-

9 Werhane, 1989.

wise, we should not try to solve all societal problems with economic tools—we will get bad solutions, even if we perfect capitalism. Other economic problems cannot be solved by capitalism because, for example, they have a natural tendency to create monopolies, nullifying the decentralizing effect of private property. Consider our road system: we cannot build massive parallel roads; therefore, private ownership of roads leads to monopolies. If a monopoly is unavoidable, the best way to mitigate negative effects is for an institution controlled by the stakeholders of the monopoly to control it. In our road example, the state (or a commons) is controlled by democracy, and it should be responsible for the construction and maintenance of our roads.

But perhaps capitalism is not as decentralizing as I suggest here. The rise of multinational corporations is surely disproving the decentralizing capabilities of capitalism! In defense of capitalism, I would like say that there are still many small- and medium-sized businesses that have actually been successful in decentralizing the economy. Also, compared to economic systems in which political powers directly control economic institutions (e.g., feudalism and communism), capitalism has actually been quite decentralizing. However, because capitalism relies on property rights, the (de)centralization of capital (economic power) is much more transparent in a capitalist economy than in feudalism or communism.

In an economic system without property rights, the economic power of people is more difficult to measure. For example, in a country with an absolute monarch, it is harder to evaluate the power of the farmer over the land they work than in a country where the farmer owns (with all given rights) the land. Therefore, the lack of transparency regarding economic power in a society without individual property ownership might be biasing one's view.[10]

Rights such as private property protect those with some economic power from those with much political power, and vice versa: anti-corruption laws protect those with some political power from those with much economic power. It would be far-fetched to assume that political and economic power have yet been completely separated, although there is no clear cause-and-effect relationship between the freedoms of politics and the economy. History has shown that economic unfreedom can cause political unfreedom and vice versa. It is tempting to initially strive for economic rather than political freedom, because economic power is, by nature, easier to decentralize than political power. Decisions that I make concerning my house (economic decisions) might not affect other people, but decisions that change the law will always affect others.

Some centralization is necessary for politics, but it is not necessary for economics. However, this does not imply that decentralization in politics is impossible or that we should strive for it less than in economics. In fact, since a chain is only as strong as the weakest link, the intricate relationship between both types of decentralization urges us to focus on political decentralization, as it is the most difficult to achieve.

10 In the absence of private property, multinational corporations would probably not exist in their current form. However, the same economic power would be combined with other powers (politics, religion, etc.) and held by monarchs or other leaders. Although these capitals might not be "owned" by those leaders (based on the current legal definition of ownership), practically it would be theirs to control.

Indeed, in their book *Why Nations Fail*,[11] Daron Acemoglu and James A. Robinson wonderfully explain why we see such a discrepancy in both prosperity and liberties in the world. They discuss as an example the differences between North and South Korea, created by both the political and economic institutions that govern those countries. In North Korea, an elite creates and maintains powerful institutions that are designed to extract wealth and perpetuate their power. In contrast, South Korea has inclusive institutions that allow broader participation and the decentralization of power in both the economy and in politics. Importantly, their book describes a process in which (inclusive/extractive) political institutions stimulate the stability of (inclusive/extractive) economic institutions. In contrast, a mix of inclusive and extractive institutions will be unstable, resulting in a drift toward either all-inclusive or all-extractive institutions.

But what if our current Western economic and political institutions are still extractive institutions—although less so than those that they have replaced? This idea would explain why many top-down multinational corporations thrive today—they have advantages in the current political system that heavily rely upon top-down political institutions (e.g., the over-centralization of political parties). The advantages of multinationals and elites are easily observed by the influence they have on politicians and their ability to direct the law. They exert influence by the creation of laws favoring multinational corporations with legal tax evasion, bailouts, and subsidies. This is often described as crony capitalism.

11 Acemoglu and Robinson, 2012.

For example, Gilens and Page (2014) tested the independent political influence of average citizens, elites, and mass-based and business-oriented interest groups. They concluded that average citizens and mass-based interest groups have little to no influence on law creation, while elites and business-oriented interest groups have substantial independent influence. Therefore, if we want to change the current crony capitalism, which is controlled by elites, to a more decentralized capitalism, we must decentralize our political institutions. This would require a stronger freedom of political entrepreneurship and application of the subsidiary principle.

I suggest that the relationship between the economy and politics could be compared to that of a dog and his owner. Just as the moral owner creates the rules for the amoral dog, so the moral politics create the rules for the amoral economic institutions. The owner keeps the dog because of the advantages it provides as a guard and companion. Ideally, the owner trains the dog to behave within specific boundaries. However, if the dog is not effectively trained by the owner, the dog might reveal unwanted behavior. Should we blame a dog, which has no morals? And is crippling the dog to prevent its unwanted behavior the best action, as this will also restrain the dog from guarding and helping the owner? Similarly, we should question politics for inadequate attempts to set clear limits for economic institutions that misbehave. The solution cannot be found in abolishing private economic institutions, as communism suggests, but in strengthening the independent political capabilities by creating laws that can set moral standards for economic institutions.

Capitalism has been beneficial for society, but there might be other viable, decentralized economic systems. However, as a supporter of piecemeal social engineering, I think improving the current system is the most preferable option. If we want to continue enjoying the benefits of capitalism, we must find ways to remove multinationals' social advantages (e.g., legal, political, and tax advantages) compared to smaller companies. Because the structures of political institutions determine how we (i.e., me, you, citizens, companies) interact with those institutions, further decentralization of democracy is probably the best way to decentralize capitalism.

5 WHAT ARE POLITICAL PARTIES?

What are political parties? This is not an essentialistic question; rather, it is a practical question that I will answer with the description I use throughout this book. Political parties are organizations with direct political power—power that they use to solve social problems. Direct political power is wielded based on a presence in parliament, the government, or any law-creating institution.

This definition is broad, in that it defines political parties as more than just groups that participate in elections. Political parties also includes organizations such as the Chinese and Russian communist parties and the German Nazi party, all of which abolished fair elections. It should be obvious to the reader that I oppose undemocratic political parties. While my definition of political parties is broader than the common definition, the references to political parties in this book will mainly refer to political parties that take part in democratic politics, as it is my aim to argue that the scope of these organizations should be reformed.

It is notable that we have different kinds of political parties in different political systems. Although the behavior of parties is mostly unpredictable, we can engineer the political systems in which these parties survive, thereby changing some of the behavior of those parties. For example, a party with competition cannot afford to make as many mistakes as a party without competition. Having a multi-party system improves parties by (a) adaption, because politicians will behave differently in the presence of competition, and (b) selection, because other (better) parties/politicians can be selected instead.

6 CRITIQUE OF POLITICAL PARTIES

Etymologically, the word "party" originates from the Latin *partiri*, which means "to divide into parts." James Madison, one of the founding fathers of the United States, warned in Federalist Papers No. 10[12] about the destructive effects of political parties, as they would divide the nation and undermine common interests. It is remarkable that the writers of the US Constitution did not foresee a function for political parties. However, since then, all modern democracies have become partisan, suggesting an essential function for parties in large political systems. This fact stands as a warning for those who try to design a political system without considering an organizational layer between individuals and the complete political system. Political parties are an essential part of democracy if nationwide policies are desired.

12 avalon.law.yale.edu/18th_century/fed10.asp

In 1902, Moisey Y. Ostrogorski published *Democracy and the Organization of Political Parties.* Ostrogorski was a Russian Jew far ahead of his time: he wrote about the equality of the sexes and actively pursued equal rights for Jews. His fierce opinions on political parties still seem very contemporary:

> This corruption of democracy had reached its highest point in England and the United States, where party had ceased to be either public, open or responsible. Parties had extended and formalized their activities by means of the caucus, the local and national organizations for the manipulation and marshaling of voters. Instead of being an ad hoc union of like minded people for the pursuit of agreed, and specific, objects, parties had replaced union with uniformity, restricting choice within the artificial dualism of a two party system, sapping and constraining the exercise of independent civic judgment and initiative, and intervening in fields where they had no business: the parliamentary elections, and the government of the state.[13]

Robert Michels was also strongly influenced by Ostrogorski, and together with Ostrogorski and Max Weber he is considered one of the founders of political sociology.[14] In 1911 he published his famous work, *Political Parties*,[15] in which he analyzed European socialist parties and trade unions. Two of his important conclusions strongly influenced this work. First, organization implies oligarchy; that is, organizations will centralize power. This is also known as the *iron law of oligarchy.* Secondly, according to Michels, socialist parties were the most democratic parties,

13 Barker and Howard-Johnston, 1975.
14 en.wikipedia.org/wiki/Moisey_Ostrogorsky, Lipset (1982)
15 Michels, 1911.

and even they created oligarchy. To Michels, this implied that democracy was impossible. This conclusion led him to later join the fascist movement in Italy.

Organizations certainly favor oligarchy, but democracy is not impossible. While creating a complete democracy within a political party is impossible, hindering the objectives of the party,[16] democracy is not a simple sum of political parties; rather, it should be considered an emergent property of the political system. It therefore depends on the number of parties and the interactions between them. Democratic parties should not be seen as organizations that aim for democracy within; they should be considered organizations that facilitate a free political landscape. This can be seen in an analogy of a free market.[17] A free market does not consist of companies maintaining free markets within their organization, but of a market that contains fairly competing companies.

Because of the undemocratic tendencies of our current political parties, a simple solution would be to remove them. Although this may seem tempting, it is completely wrong. Organizations are essential building blocks that are required when systems are large and complex. They represent choices, and they catalyze subsequent realizations. In a sense, political parties can be compared to the instincts of humans. Because humans have many instincts, we are

16 Much like the socialist party in Michels' life, the Pirate Party, a political party that originated in Sweden and focuses on online rights, has attempted in some countries to maximize its internal democracy. I have been active in the Belgian Pirate Party and have observed both the merits and disadvantages of these attempts.

17 A free market here refers to one free from all forms of economic privilege, monopolies, and artificial scarcities, not laissez-faire economics. en.wikipedia.org/wiki/Free_market#Geoist_Economics

mentally free compared to lower animals, which have fewer instincts, or plants, which have none. The fewer instincts, the more influence of each remaining individual instinct. Ideas to eliminate political parties make the same mistake that communism made by trying to eliminate private businesses.[18] By nationalising the monopolistic companies, the communists made their citizens dependent on only one monopolistic state-company.

7 CHANGING POLITICAL PARTIES

Our political systems are not truly democratic, because they are controlled by a limited number of political parties; therefore, a small group of leaders and other (e.g., economic) elites who influence those leaders control our political systems. In order to democratize this system, the party system must be decentralized. I will outline in Chapters 2 and 3 how this can be accomplished. The most important step of this process is to increase the number of parties and to decrease the size of the current parties.

How many parties are ideal? Let us consider two other types of organizations: companies and non-governmental organizations (NGOs). Amar Prabhu estimates that there are 115,000,000 companies in the world,[19] and the number of NGOs has been estimated by Michal Alter to be 10,000,000[20]. According to the CIA factbook there are

18 Ideas to eliminate political parties cannot work in large-scale democracies. However, smaller political bodies (towns or small cities) might be able to do without parties.

19 www.quora.com/How-many-companies-exist-in-the-world

20 www.quora.com/Non-Governmental-Organizations-NGOs-How-many-nonprofits-are-there-in-the-world

between 1,000 and 10,000 political parties worldwide.[21] Using these numbers, there is only one political party per 1,000 NGOs or 10,000 companies. I think the number of political parties should increase by at least a hundredfold.

This may seem like an unrealistic expansion. After all, who will create and maintain all these new political parties? However, most of these organizations already exist—although they are not yet political parties. We should change the rules by which political organizations can act as political parties; this will transform many NGOs into political parties. The rules that determine which political organizations can be political parties are too restrictive. By adopting more flexible rules, a larger fraction of civil society will be able to directly control the political system. This will change the number of political parties and, subsequently, the behavior of political parties, as they will more closely resemble the current NGOs (see Figure 1.1). For example, these parties will become more specialized and less reliant on ideology (see Chapter 2).

The huge increase in political parties will undoubtedly make it impossible for any person to fully comprehend the complete system.[22] People tend to evaluate complex systems as unachievable when they cannot completely comprehend the system mechanics. This is often correct, especially for top-down designs that require an omniscient designer who needs to anticipate the outcomes of the system. In contrast, bottom-up designs are based on local corrections and, therefore, it is not necessary to know all outcomes of the complete system. Bottom-up systems are

21 www.cia.gov/library/publications/the-world-factbook/fields/2118.html

22 I would argue that the current "understanding" of systems with few parties is just an illusion.

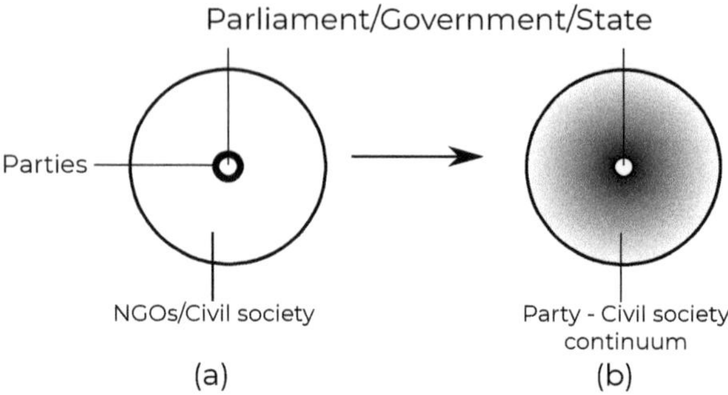

FIGURE 1.1: Transition to a decentralized party system. Before the transition **(a)**, we observe a distinction between political organizations with (parties) and without direct political power (NGOs, civil society). After the transition **(b)**, a continuum of political organizations with various degrees of direct political power (degree of blackness) will emerge. Therefore, the power that political parties currently possess will be distributed among many more organizations.

very viable, even if the complete system is not understood. There are many examples of bottom-up systems; I will describe one natural system (multicellular organisms) and two artificially created systems (the free market and crowdsourced projects, e.g. Linux and Wikipedia).

First, multicellular organisms, such as humans, are considered to be so complex and wondrous in their structure and function that many believe a supernatural designer must have some role in their creation. While no one completely understands how human bodies work, the combined bottom-up information processing of cells ensures that human bodies function.

The free market is another example of a bottom-up system. Jonas Eliasson, in his interesting TED talk,[23] narrates the story of a Russian communist who asked an English urban planner in 1989, "who is in charge of London's bread supply?" For the communist, it was unimaginable that no one was in charge of the complicated system of bread supply, while the Englishmen simply answered that it organizes itself.

Finally, in the twentieth century, large projects like Linux[24] and Wikipedia[25] were decentralized; this had previously been considered only attainable by a centralized organization. Although these examples provide no guarantees about the viability of the political system described in this book, they do offer some assurance (to me at least) that bottom-up solutions can be used to improve our current political system.

8 THE FLAWS OF POLITICAL PARTIES

It is often hard to "see" freedom when we are so used to having our freedoms restricted. For example, many consider Western democracy to be a free political system. I argue that this is not the case. These democracies are notable for containing relatively few political parties, and those parties have oligopolistic power. It is very difficult to create new parties that can successfully and directly achieve political actions. Because of this inability for direct political action, many political organizations are forced to use indirect means to achieve their goals, such as protests,

23 www.youtube.com/watch?v=CX_Krxq5eUI
24 Raymond, 1999.
25 Giles, 2005.

strikes, and judicial actions. However, these actions often seem ineffective, and the resulting frustrations and misuse of democratic institutions result in undermined trust in democracy and the growing support of demagogues.

The "unfreedom" created in these democracies is an indirect effect of the exclusivity of political parties. We can find concrete examples of this exclusivity in voting legislation that restricts voters to one representative or party at a time. We can also see this in parliament, where each representative is bound to one political party. I will address both situations in the following chapters. This exclusivity rule is advantageous for political parties that aim to achieve greater power over both citizens and representatives in parliament; however, it is, and has been, disastrous for individual political freedoms and for society as a whole.

CHAPTER 2

EXCLUSIVE PARTIES

1 OSTROGORKSKI'S LOST HOPE

To decentralize the political party system, we should reduce the requirements for a civil organization to become a political party. Ostrogorkski already envisioned a similar idea in his political work, *Democracy and the Organization of Political Parties.* In 1902, a reviewer for the *New York Times* described Ostrogorski's book:

> The solution of the problem, both in England and America, must be, according to M. Ostrogorski, the cessation of the use of permanent parties with power as their end. Party must become once more a combination of citizens formed specially for a particular issue. In other words, the fundamental political principle must be Union instead of unity.[1]

However, Ostrogorski gave few suggestions about how to change from a system with parties. He thought the changes were inevitable, as described by the reviewer:

> The old parties, though still bearing the traditional names, are crumbling. In this country the tendency toward free homogeneous associations is seen in the formation of Commitees of seventy, Leagues, civic Federations, Citizens' Movements ... [Ostrogorski] makes no suggestions as to the means by which the desired change is to be brought about, but it may be inferred that he

1 *The Party System: Ostrogorski's Work on Democracy and Political Organisation (review)*, 1902

> believes the pressure of necessity will be sufficient to strengthen the influence of temporary leagues and thus bring about the decline and fall of permanent parties.[2]

Despite Ostrogorski's hopes, political parties did not fade away. They became even stronger, as the Communist and Nazi parties were going to influence politics in the century to come. Ostrogorski's hopes were false!

This disconnect between Ostrogorski's hopes and reality may be why Ostrogorski has been almost completely ignored by political theorists for more than a century. He was even ridiculed—for example, by Seymour M. Lipset:

> And I would suggest that one reason why [Robert] Michels has been more influential than Ostrogorski is that the German sociologist did not leave himself open to the charge of naïvity or inconsistency. Many discussions of Ostrogorski pay tribute to his analytical or descriptive insights, and then conclude by triumphantly demonstrating how patently ridiculous are his proposed reforms.

It is undoubtedly true that Ostrogorski posed a bold hypothesis. But those who ridiculed him were blind to his suggestions because they were unable to see beyond the dogmas of the political party. Examples of how others failed to see beyond these dogmas will follow (e.g., a party needs ideology).

More then a hundred years later, we find ourselves in a similar situation. While citizens seem to be smarter and more connected than ever, it would be foolish to think that

2 *The Party System: Ostrogorski's Work on Democracy and Political Organisation (review)*, 1902

parties will now make space for their replacements. In this work, I aim to investigate what fundamentally differentiates parties from other political organizations. With this understanding, the transformation of parties comes within our reach. Parties acquire direct power via elections, have opinions about multiple political problems, and are exclusive. In contrast, NGOs have opinions on specific political problems, do not take part in elections, and are inclusive.

What is political party exclusivity? *Party exclusivity* means that if you are a member/voter in one political party, then you cannot be a member/voter in another political party. Exclusivity grants a political party power over a person; because in general, exclusivity reduces the person's freedom, it should be used as seldom as possible. However, exclusivity can sometimes be a good thing, such as in cases when a person has a lot of power (e.g., public mandates should not be combined with other—private—interests or accumulated with other public mandates) or in cases when exclusivity is symmetric (e.g., spouses can demand mutual exclusivity).[3]

The use of inclusivity/exclusivity in this book refers to mutual inclusivity/exclusivity between parties in particular, although other organizations or groups can be included. For example, joining a party will restrict me from joining other parties, but I can still join a sports fan club. However, organizations can also associate with political parties, which can confer exclusivity to the citizens or members who are similarly politically affiliated. The ex-

3 Exclusivity is also described by Taleb, specifically as it relates to companies legally owning a person and the difference between monotheistic and polytheistic religions. See "How to Legally Own Another Person," Taleb, 2018.

treme of this exclusivity can be found in totalitarian societies as well as in pillarized systems in which societies were segregated by school, media consumption, sport clubs, and others.

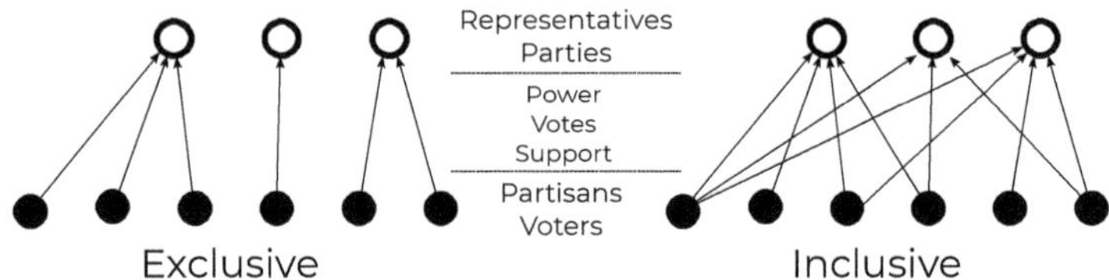

FIGURE 2.1: Differences between exclusive and inclusive party systems. Power is granted by voters and partisans to the parties by public support, active participation, or voting.

How do we abolish the exclusivity rule? We allow people to simultaneously join multiple political parties and vote for multiple parties. Then, multiple parties can represent the same individual, but each party will represent a smaller and more specific set of ideas that voters can support. Through the rest of this work, I will refer to this system as the *inclusive party system.* A more detailed description of the possible voting systems is given in Chapter 3. In the inclusive system, exclusive parties are still possible (e.g., parties could exclude members of specific parties), but complete exclusivity will put them at a disadvantage, as they must then answer all political questions (while others do not). Further, an exclusive party will have a smaller network, because their supporters cannot join other parties.

Expanding on the idea of the inclusive party system, the primary theory of this book is as follows: *Political parties in a representative democracy are currently constrained by an artificial*[4] *mutual exclusivity within elections, party statutes, and parliaments. By removing the constraints of exclusivity, political parties will become inclusive, and other political organizations of civil society will be able to become political parties.*[5] *This will result in a more decentralized political system.*

While my proposed theory and aims are similar to Ostrogorski's, his focus on political change stressed the restriction of political parties in time[6] and scope. I argue that the main goal should first be to convert parties from exclusivity to inclusivity (and create compatible parliaments/elections). Consequently, parties will become more focused on single issues (depending on the necessary popular support for a given subject) and more fragile (which will result in a more dynamic political landscape).

2 HOW THE EXCLUSIVITY RULE CREATES AN ELECTORAL OLIGOPOLY

One of the first effects of the exclusivity rule is that political parties must have opinions on all political issues. An economic example clarifies how this works. Suppose everyone in society can choose one store to shop in for every four years. You will be able to buy everything the store

4 Artificial has no moral implications. However, it does imply that these rules can be changed by people, since they were initially created by people.

5 Although they will become parties, these new parties will hardly resemble the current ones. This can be compared to a local store and a multinational corporation: both are businesses, yet they hardly resemble each other.

6 While restrictions in time are very robust in decentralizing, they can also be very impractical for long-term objectives.

sells. But there is a catch: once you have chosen your store, you will not be allowed to buy from any other stores for the next four years. In other words, the store has exclusivity over its customers for each four-year term. What will the consequences be? Well, consumers will choose the best store for them. But more importantly, consumers will choose stores that have the largest selection of goods and services. If they need any other goods during the next four years, they will not be able to purchase them. This will result in an economic landscape with a few large stores that stock as many types of goods as possible.

When we convert this idea to politics, we see that exclusivity results in a few large political parties that have opinions on all political themes. These effects are widespread: political parties become long-lived and too big to fail. "Too big to fail" is usually used to describe economic institutions whose failure poses a systemic risk because of their size and connections. In this context, it is used to describe political parties that are both large and connected with many interest groups. Even if a political party fails, the party will maintain support because there is no alternative—voters may fear that the lost influence could be claimed by a political opponent. Because political parties are not easily replaceable, they are more prone to risk (corruption, deceit, etc.) as they pursue their own interests, and they cannot be punished with replacement. In short, they are anti-fragile relative to our democracy, which makes our democracy more fragile, because society has to account for the risks parties take on. This is much like the banks that are too big to fail and are therefore able to take risks that society has to pay for when they are bailed out.

Strikingly, some political scientists see this as a beneficial property. For example, Seymour M. Lipset wrote:

> The uncritical permanent loyalty to parties, akin to religious affiliation, that Ostrogorski bemoaned, may also be viewed as contributing to the stability of the democratic process. If a significant segment of a party's electors is not uncritically loyal, crises, policy mistakes, or malfeasance by officeholders could so alienate the supporters of a party that the party would disappear as an electoral or parliamentary opposition from one to another.[7]

Lipset acknowledges that parties are too big too fail—therefore, we should just accept corrupt and incompetent political leaders, much as we accepted the atrocities of bankers in 2008. It is almost as if Lipset did not even read Ostrogorski's comments on political monopolies:

> At the same time it gave it, under cover of the formalist principle of ``regularity," the electoral monopoly. That monopoly put the public interest at the mercy of the party, or rather of the Organization which claimed to represent it. And the Organization, composed in great proportion of greedy mercenaries, systematically exploited that interest. Administration and legislation were prostituted to the Machine.[8]

How can we be sure that parties are pushed by the exclusive system to have opinions on all issues? Maybe people want to create parties with opinions on all issues. I don't think so. Although some parties might seek opinions on all issues, there is a selection process that forces new parties to become broad issue parties; otherwise they

7 Ostrogorski and Lipset, 1982, Vol II, p. lxii.
8 Ostrogorski, 1902, Vol II, p. 572.

disappear. Consider the green parties, socialist parties, and, more recently, pirate parties. They were founded to deal with very specific problems: pollution, misuse of laborers, and digital rights. Taleb suggests that instead of only looking at the survivors (the current parties), we should also look into the "graveyard of failures" to understand which characteristics are selected for.[9] There, we can observe parties that were killed by the exclusive rule because they did not adopt a broad party program. In the United States, these dead parties include the Anti-Masonic Party, the Free Soil Party, the Greenback Party, the Native American Party, and the Silver Party. These were all single-issue parties that were killed by the exclusivity rule when they were unable to transform into a many-issue party.

Countries with proportional voting systems[10] tend to be more forgiving of specialized political parties. Multiple explanations could explain this characteristic. For example, because parties can elect representatives with less popular support, smaller parties are more viable, even without a broad party program. Additionally, the parties in a proportional voting system must usually cooperate to form a government or a majority for law creation. This allows them to have more complementary specializations. For example, in the Netherlands, which uses a proportional voting system, there are more specialized parties—e.g., a party for animal welfare and a party for pensioners' interests.

9 Taleb, 2007, Chapter 8.

10 These are voting systems in which parties get X% of the elected representatives when X% of the electorate vote for them.

3 ENTRY OF POLITICAL PARTIES

In 2006, Chris Anderson published *The Long Tail: Why the Future of Business Is Selling less of More*,[11] in which he explained how, in markets with a very low entry threshold, products with very low demand (the long tail) can collectively account for a very large sales volume. In music sales, for example, although the hits account for a large portion of total sales, platforms with almost infinite shelf space (e.g., iTunes) allow niches to become increasingly important. These niches have growing popularity because a growing number of suppliers and consumers create and consume niche products. In these markets, the relative importance of the hits is reduced.

Applying this concept to party systems can explain some properties of the exclusive party system. It also allows us to make some predictions about an inclusive party system. The exclusive system is characterized by a high threshold for viability because opinions on all political issues are required. Therefore, only a few parties (the hits) will be viable. In contrast, the inclusive party system does not require opinions on all issues, lowering the threshold for party viability. With lower threshold, more political parties will emerge to fill policy niches. The number of political participants and voters will also increase as more people are persuaded by parties to address their specific needs. Finally, the relative importance of larger parties within the political system will decrease.

11 Anderson, 2006.

4 SPECIALIZATION OF POLITICS

Adam Smith suggested that divisions of labor are limited by the size of the market.[12] As the market gets bigger, labor can be further divided; therefore, the sub-units can be more specialized. The theory of John Tyler Bonner goes one step further with a size-complexity rule: as entities get bigger, they need greater complexity to be sustainable.[13] Complexity is defined, by Bonner, as the specialization of sub-units.

Bonner illustrates this phenomenon in various domains of life. For example, large multi-cellular organisms have more types of cellular specialization. Outside the realm of biology, this phenomenon can also be observed in civilization: larger societies will have more types of craftsmen. Increased specialization also implies that these sub-units are dependent on each other and that more interactions will occur. Specialization in complex systems is not merely permissible in greater sizes—it is a necessity!

The increased specialization required for larger entities also explains why political institutions that are perfectly suitable for towns and small cities might not be effective in larger entities like countries, or even in super-national entities like the EU. The size of our democratic entities has increased; they encompass more land and larger populations. Concurrently, more people have been able to participate as a result of universal suffrage. Our problem is not so much finding *the* democratic system—as if there were one best democratic system that fits all sizes—but rather finding democratic systems that work for larger so-

12 Smith, 1776, Book I, Chapter 3.
13 Bonner, 2004.

cieties. Small societies can easily remain democratic and egalitarian without complex rules. For example, one rule of pirate parties requires local crews to be small enough that all members can meet at one table—a simple heuristic to keep a group democratic. Propositions to implement a political system that was successfully applied to smaller groups of citizens (e.g., ancient Athens[14]) are unlikely to work as intended in large, modern states.

More importantly, the current party system is completely inadequate to satisfy the level of specialization required in our society. There are two distinct ways political parties could satisfy the needed complexity: (a) many specialized parties, or (b) few parties made of many specialized sub-units. However, neither option seems viable in the current political system. The first option, as explained before, is not compatible with the exclusive party system, because the exclusivity rule forces parties to maintain a wide spectrum of opinions, obstructing specialization (see Section 2 in this chapter). The latter system, with a few internally specialized parties, is compatible with the exclusive party system. However, it is unclear whether individual parties are, in themselves, large enough to provide all needed specializations. This is even more questionable for countries where the membership of parties is steadily decreasing.[15] However, regardless of whether political parties can provide the needed specializations, the size-complexity rule demands sufficient specialization at a certain size. Rather than being provided by political parties, these specializations are now provided by NGOs, think tanks, and corporate lobbyists. However, outsourcing political specializations comes at a price.

14 Van Reybrouck, 2013.
15 Van Biezen, Mair, and Poguntke, 2012.

Consider these examples of outsourcing from Belgium, described by Luc Huyse in his book *De democratie voorbij* (*Beyond the Democracy*).[16] Huyse first describes the increased importance of an organized social society. Via committees, these organizations are increasingly more involved in legislative processes. Although this may seem a welcome change since it weakens the oligopolistic power of political parties, it comes with great concerns. One of the most important features of democracy was stated by Karl Popper: the peaceful transition of power by elections; this can be broadly interpreted as the power of the people to dismiss elites.[17] However, there are no elections for the NGOs that exercise power through these committees, and they may become impossible to remove.

In Belgium there is an additional oligopolistic concern about NGOs that have originated from political pillarization. Pillarization is the segregation of society along ideological segments; it occurred in Belgium in the late nineteenth and first half of the twentieth century. This segregation has since eroded, but non-profit organizations formed during that period still largely dominate their field of activity.[18] Examples of these NGOs are trade unions and health maintenance organizations (*mutualiteiten*): there is a Catholic, liberal, and socialist organization for each. Some of these NGOs are only associated with one specific pillar: e.g., the largest farmer organization and the organization that represents small businesses are most strongly linked with the Catholic pillar. All of these NGOs strongly dominate their territory, often by political connections or

16 Huyse, 2014
17 Popper, 1945, Vol I, Ch. 7.
18 Huyse, 2014; Vogels, 2014

privileges granted by law, and they cannot be challenged by elections.

The second way society fills the political vacuum of specializations originates from economic organizations. The capitalistic economy has been very successful at specializing; therefore, it is very capable of providing the needed information to politicians. However, by doing so, the information provided to politicians is often biased toward the interests of economic elites (such as the financial backer of the specialist), and barriers between economic and political power are broken down.

Current political parties are incapable of providing the necessary specializations required by larger societies. This results in the dependence of politicians on external organizations that, unlike parties, are not subject to public control by elections. To reclaim control by the people, political parties must be more independent of other forces. More specialized parties can be created (if need be, by converting NGOs to parties); otherwise, greater specialization is needed in the current parties. However, when we consider the different types of specialization, it seems to me that the specialization of political parties as a whole—not of their sub-units—is the more effective solution.

5 TOP-DOWN VS BOTTOM-UP SPECIALIZATION

Specialization is the process by which sub-units focus on a specific problem in order to increase the likelihood of solving that specific problem. Thereby, these sub-units become more dependent on each other since they require other sub-units to solve problems they are not capable to solve.

There are two types of specialization: bottom-up and top-down. Examples of top-down specialization include different departments in a large corporation (information technology, human resources, public relations, etc.) or academia (sciences, literature, social sciences, etc.). An authority creates the specialized categories in top-down specialization. Top-down specialization is characterized by exclusivity, limited redundancy, inflexibility, and fragility. It becomes fragile because choices about the number of sub-units and the delineation of categories influences how people can specialize. Wrong assumptions and requirements for new specializations can damage the system. For example, in a company with financial and IT departments, who should specialize in the use of digital currencies (e.g., bitcoin)? In academia, this problem is being partially addressed with the creation of interdisciplinary roles. Although top-down specialization is often efficient, redundancies are more likely to be wastfull because those who specialize are less able to innovate or to specialize in new requirements.

In contrast, bottom-up specialization is characterized by a tolerance of redundancy, flexibility, inclusivity, and anti-fragility. The sub-unit determines its specialization. Two examples clearly exhibit this phenomenon: spaghetti sales and gene function. If I want to buy spaghetti on a regular day, I will probably buy it in a general local grocery. If I want to cook a special type of spaghetti, I might go to a grocery that specializes in Italian products. However, if I conceived this plan too late in the evening, my only way to purchase spaghetti is to go to a convenience store.[19] While all three options are specialized in selling spaghetti (redundancy), they are also uniquely specialized in a niche. There are no fixed boundaries for specialization, and subunits can change their specialization as needed for them to survive. If one of the three options should fail for me, there are still two other options.

The second example of bottom-up specialization is gene specialization. The human genome contains about 25,000 genes; almost all have a different specialization. However, many genes have very similar *sibling* genes that arise during gene duplication events. Gene duplication occurs when a single gene or a whole chromosome, containing thousands of genes, is duplicated, giving rise to identical copies. This redundancy allows these genes to mutate without detriment to the next generation. In this way, new functions are explored by changing the time, place, and conditions of expression, or by affecting the chemical structure of the gene product. For example, humans have seven different hemoglobin genes[20] (α, β, γ, δ, ϵ, π, and ζ) that all originated from the same ancestral gene—this has allowed for specific embryonic and fetal hemoglobins, which have a slightly altered role from that of the adult.[21] Similar to an economy in which most entrepreneurs fail to succeed with a new business, most duplicated genes fail to specialize in a new function and eventually disappear. Genetic redundancy does not only originate from duplicated genes; independent chemical pathways can also perform the same

19 In Belgium, with the exception of these convenience stores, shops are closed at night.

20 Hemoglobin proteins transport oxygen in the blood.

21 D. Voet, J. G. Voet, and Pratt, 2013, Section 5-4B.

function in a cell, creating redundancy.[22] Susumu Ohno popularized the notion that gene duplication creates redundancy, which in turn enables biological innovation.[23]

Returning to the question of whether we should have (a) many specialized parties or (b) few parties with many specialized sub-units, it seems that the former option favors bottom-up specialization while the latter favors top-down. Many specialized parties will directly compete with each other, requiring individual decisions by those parties. In contrast, specialized sub-units of different parties will not have to directly compete with each other. Because their survival primarily depends on the survival of the party, the party authority will determine the specialization of their sub-units.

As an economic example, consider a corporate canteen and a privately owned restaurant. Both the canteen and restaurant provide food. But the restaurant competes with other restaurants in the neighborhood, while the canteen has no competition within the corporation. Therefore, the success of the restaurant is determined by competition with other restaurants. In contrast, the canteen will be supported as long as the corporation survives. Decisions about food, price, and atmosphere are decided only by the restaurant, while for the canteen, decisions must fit within corporate guidelines.

Is it impossible for a large party system to develop bottom-up specializations? No, but it requires democracy within the party—a difficult goal to achieve, as already

22 Zhang, 2012.
23 Ohno, 1970.

noted by Robert Michels.[24] Therefore, we should pursue an inclusive party system that will create many small, specialized parties. These parties might be somewhat redundant, but they will make our political system more flexible, innovative, and anti-fragile.

6 COMPETITION AND COOPERATION

Some people have said that competition should keep our political parties in line—an idea that I completely endorse. But I ask: is there sufficient competition? In Belgium there are socialist, liberal, and green parties. To return to our spaghetti/supermarket analogy, there is hardly any competition because the three choices populate a different niche. If real competition is desired, multiple political parties must be specialized within the same niche. However, the exclusive party system does not allow such competition. Multiple parties within the same niche weakens the power of those combined parties because they have to split support among them. Furthermore, because of the high entrance threshold for parties, it is very hard for new competitors to be viable.

The exclusive party system is characterized by zero-sum politics—every gain in influence by one party (voters or representatives) is only possible due to a loss by another. This principle is called zero-sum because the sum of influence differences is always zero. This forces exclusive political parties to be more competitive and less cooperative.

---

24 Michels, 1911.

In contrast, an inclusive party system is not restricted by zero-sum politics. Because parties can share influence over individuals, cooperation is much more widespread. Paradoxically, although more similar parties gain influence (they have a lower start-up threshold) and increase the overall competition, the cooperation between similar parties will also increase because they can share participants and goals. As a YouTube viewer, I observe the same phenomenon. Although YouTube has immensely lowered the threshold for content creators, thereby increasing competition, there is also an astonishing amount of cooperation between content creators, all of whom are trying to improve their own content. This is only possible because YouTube views are not a zero-sum game. More views for one creator's channel does not necessarily result in a decrease in views for another channel. Instead, viewers can spend more total time watching YouTube, benefiting cooperating content creators. Political parties are, in a sense, political content creators.

Additionally, we must distinguish competition and cooperation at both the party and individual levels. In an exclusive system, having more parties increases competition, at the expense of cooperation between both parties and individuals. In the inclusive system, having more parties increases both competition and cooperation at the party level. The inclusive system also increases the likelihood that people with a shared goal participate and cooperate in the same party. See Figure 2.2; this graph clearly shows why an exclusive party system will inevitably lead to a zero-sum game for parties: a person with allegiance to one party cannot be a part of another. In contrast, a person in an inclusive system can be part of multiple parties, which might even benefit all those parties because information can therefore quickly flow from one group to another.

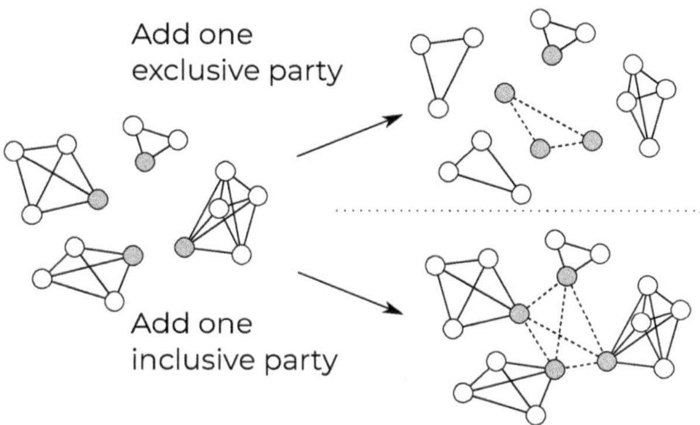

FIGURE 2.2: Adding one party increases competition for parties in both inclusive and exclusive systems. Inclusive systems allow more cooperation (edges) between individuals (nodes; grey nodes have a common issue), because the additional party (subgraphs) facilitates connections with people. In contrast, the addition of an exclusive party can only reduce cooperation between people—edges are destroyed to establish a new party.

In 1954, Muzafer Sherif described an experiment in group conflict.[25] He showed that by creating groups with randomly assigned members and letting those groups contest each other in different camp games, he could increase intra-group cohesion while decreasing inter-group cohesion. The random assignment of the test subjects into exclusive groups had real life consequences on the test subjects, reinforcing the exclusive groups into which they were arbitrary assigned. This might explain why the current exclusive parties feel as if they are the result of an inevitable social process. Indeed, the same in-group favoritism can be ob-

25 Sherif et al., 1954.

served between partisan groups, and it has been suggested that this causes discrimination in the United States to a degree that even exceeds racial discrimination.[26] This is problematic, because it reduces the ability of partisans to see problems from alternative viewpoints and to reach consensus to solve social problems. How can we reverse these tendencies of group conflict in politics?

One solution is to create a supergroup that includes the members of all groups. However, it is extremely unlikely that all members will voluntarily participate. Another more viable solution is to abolish exclusivity. Exclusivity hinders the development of multiple political identities and, thus, participation in different groups. We observe polarization in new democracies with underdeveloped inclusive civil societies that are dominated by exclusive groups. This polarization adds to the often difficult conditions of those new democracies, sometimes resulting in civil wars or a return to autocracy. Some contemporary examples include the civil war in Iraq (Sunni vs. Shia), the Arab Spring in Egypt (secular vs. non-secular), and the Rwandan genocide (Hutu vs. Tutsi). In each of these examples, political polarization has been observed between religious and/or ethnic groups, and political parties have failed to counteract polarization.

However, it would be naive to think that only new democracies are subject to this problem. Belgium is also politically polarized by exclusive parties that cater to Dutch or French speakers, and in Northern Ireland, the biggest political conflict features polarization between Irish Nationalists and Unionists. The top-down peace obtained by the leaders of these exclusive groups is only temporary if

26 Iyengar and Westwood, 2015.

the people remain separated from each other by these exclusive parties. Although citizens of different groups (religions, ethnicities, etc.) may have different opinions on some subjects, as a result of the exclusive political parties they will remain segregated from each other, even if they share opinions on other subjects. Because those citizens are segregated, they are less likely to empathize with those from other groups. Exclusive parties, therefore, reinforce divides that are already present.

7 FRAGILITY OF THE EXCLUSIVE PARTY SYSTEM

I have discussed how the exclusive party system constrains political parties and causes them to become multi-issue parties. When a party is supported by a group of citizens for a specific theme, it also has the authority to achieve other aims, which might include hidden but severe risks. This occurs because the exclusive party understands its successful election as a mandate to accomplish all parts of its platform. Or in Ostrogorski's words:

> [Political parties] stereotype opinion in creeds which enforce on it a rigid discipline, they conceal the divergence of views that arise by composite programmes in which the most varied problems are jumbled together, which promise everything to everybody, which reconcile contradiction by rhetoric artifices, masterpieces of shuffling and humbug. Those electors who are in agreement with the party on a single point of its programme only are obliged, in order to get that point carried, to vote for all the rest, in spite of their convictions.[27]

27 Ostrogorski, 1902, Vol II, p656-657.

For example, a certain party might have a good economic plan and could thereby become the leading party during an economic crisis. However, perhaps this party also supports an abominable environmental policy that damages society. Citizens may vote for the party because they support its economic plan; it is unclear whether they also support its environmental agenda. The exclusive party system is therefore fragile with regard to the evaluation of party programs by the electorate. Consider also the observed fragility of the exclusive party system toward populists. Populists will often reduce many political problems to one single problem (e.g. capitalism, nationalism, or immigration), ignoring the complexity of many problems. Although there may be valid reasons to examine this one problem, upon election, populists also gain power over all political issues in the exclusive system.

It is also necessary for these multi-issue parties to form a coalition when they lack a majority by themselves. A majority coalition will provide shared power for parties in the coalition, relative to a minority, for all political issues. The outcome of the system then greatly depends on how the parties are comprised. The combination of two ideologically identical parties with 30 percent of the electorate will not give the same outcome as only one party of 60 percent, although both options represent the same electorate. In the former, a coalition, which can fail, is required, while the party with 60 percent does not need to form a coalition. Coalitions are created by the leaders of parties; therefore, preliminary agreements between parties, or affection and intrigues between party leaders, might also seriously impact the political outcome of a country. For example, if three parties are supported by 33 percent of the electorate each, any combination of two parties can form a coalition with more than 50 percent. But these coalition formations are often very unpredictable, and the electorate cannot directly influence them. The exclusive party system is therefore fragile regarding the composition of parties and the decisions of their leaders when making coalitions.

A specific example of the fragility of the exclusive party system is the rise to power of the Nazi party. Its twenty-five-point program[28] was clearly intended to benefit the working class (e.g., expansion of elderly welfare, profit-sharing in large industries) [29]. However, its racist, totalitarian, and war-mongering proposals had a much greater impact on the world than its pro-labor ideas. An inclusive system would likely have isolated the pro-labor sentiments, enabling the realization of positive proposals without genocide, a world war, or tyranny. Extremist organizations can damage society, but they can only become totalitarian when they achieve significant power (e.g., via an exclusive party). The Nazi party, by itself, never actually obtained an absolute majority in the Bundestag. It was only in 1932, after a period of intrigues, that a coalition formed between the Centre party, led by Franz von Papen, and the Nazi party, consolidating Adolf Hitler's power. Without that coalition, history might have looked very different. This illustrates the fragility of the choices leaders make in an exclusive party system.

28 en.wikipedia.org/wiki/National_Socialist_Program#The_25-point_-Program_of_the_NSDAP as on 28/12/2007

29 Indeed, the rise to power of the Nazi party was probably only achievable by the support of many Communists and Socialists. They were referred to as Beefsteak Nazis, as they were brown on the outside but red within. See en.wikipedia.org/wiki/Beefsteak_Nazi

Belgian politicians have adopted a strategy called *cordon sanitair*: never form coalitions with extreme (right) parties. However, it is difficult for citizens to evaluate parties without power because they cannot make real mistakes. Therefore, these extreme parties might appear to citizens over time as good alternatives. Therefore, the longer these parties are without power, the easier it is for them to gain power. Then, when a crisis suddenly appears, people are more likely to vote for riskier choices, which could result in the complete victory of extremists—a Black Swan. The real solution to this problem is not to restrict extremists from gaining any power; rather, all parties should be generally restricted (including the extreme) from gaining too much power. The inclusive party system achieves this by narrowing the scope of parties as they specialize. Furthermore, parties can be restricted by the power they have in the legislative process (see the next chapter).

Other factors that reveal the fragility of the exclusive party system are the quality of the leaders and experts upon whom they rely, the involvement of foreign powers (e.g., hacking of the US Democratic National Committee in 2016), and the involvement of religious and economic leaders.

8 IDEOLOGY

The Pirate Party is a political party formed in Sweden that initially focused on internet freedoms (intellectual property, privacy, censorship, transparency, etc.). In the 2014 elections for the European Parliament, the Swedish Pirates lost two seats; the German Pirates were the only pirate party to win even a single position. I suspect many Pi-

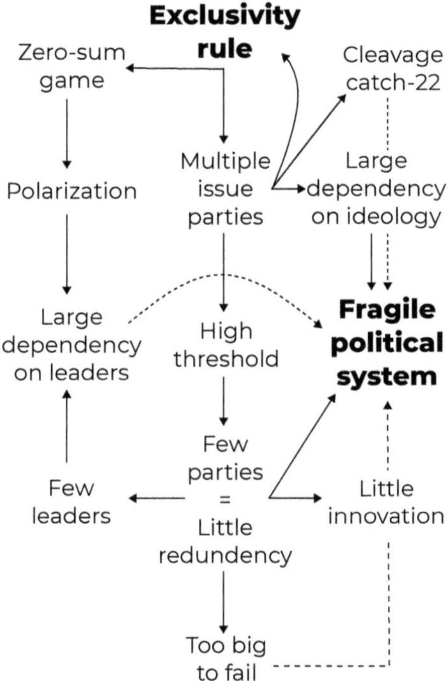

FIGURE 2.3: Impact of the exclusivity of political parties on the political system. Note the feedback loop of multiple issue parties caused by the exclusivity rule; creating a one-dimensional political landscape reinforces itself.

rates were disappointed, including Peter Sunde, a political activist best known as the co-founder and spokesperson of The Pirate Bay. Because I hold him in such high regard, I will use his writing as an example to explain a widely believed misconception. In 2015 he wrote an essay entitled "The Pirate Movement is Dead"[30] in which he stated that it would be better for Pirates to abandon their ambitions of a political party and join other parties in order to spread their ideas more effectively:

> In the essence of what a pirate means today -- I'm talking the political pirate -- I'm all in. But I'm also so much more and I hope you guys are as well. I hope you care about the bigger picture. The ``pirate movement" does not have space for that though. So why would you limit yourself to that? Why would you spend your energy and time on something that has no working big picture? It's a subset of politics that the ``movement" has been dealing with. And that's fine, but not in the form of a party. A party needs to be able to have that ideological big picture view. Who can say what the ``pirate movement's" view on immigration is? Or the war against drugs and so on? It would be different in each country. There's no alignment here.

Sunde believes ideologies are essential for political parties. However, this is an example of survival bias—most successful parties indeed have an ideology, but political parties do not require ideologies. Some parties have adopted ideologies and subsequently gained an electoral advantage for having them. Ideologies are powerful tools for creating a convincing narrative and more efficiently seeking a consensus on the full scope of political issues. Since exclusive political parties must have opinions on a range of issues, an ideology is a powerful tool to find a consensus on all

30 torrentfreak.com/peter-sunde-the-pirate-movement-is-dead-150404/

these different problems.[31] Single-issue parties, like those found in the graveyard of failures,[32] rely much less on an ideology, but they do not survive in the exclusive system.

Other methods of finding consensus rely on a charismatic leader or other authoritative source (e.g., the Bible). But charismatic leaders cannot lead forever. In contrast, a model or theory can survive passage through time, from generation to generation. Instead of seeking agreement on each separate issue, it is far more efficient to agree on a model and then to try to generate solutions for the different problems with the agreed model. However, when a party strictly follows a model, they inevitably form extreme ideas when the model does not fit the world or sensible morals (e.g., communists, Nazis, and ISIS).[33] Parties that do acknowledge the restrictions of their model will adapt it, add more models, or find a consensus that deviates from their model.

In an inclusive party system with many specific small parties, models are less valuable because parties become more problem oriented. Different models can still be valid for a certain problem, but these models become less important for the survival of the party. For example, a party formed to support the preservation of forests could be defended from an ecological (the forest has ecological value), nationalist (the forest symbolizes national pride), or religious (sacred ground) standpoint. Therefore, more people's views can be represented. People have multiple identities and multiple (sometimes seemingly inconsistent)

31 Or it is misused, by the elite, to justify/frame their decisions.

32 see Section 2

33 A good reference on how the political model of South African Apartheid deviated from reality is Derman, 2011.

opinions that cannot be combined in a single political organization or ideology.

Models are best used as a tool for a specific problem—not to forward or solve the Big Picture—and with a better understanding of the model's limits. While current ideologies seem very anti-fragile—people keep defending them, even when all evidence refutes them—new models with limited scope could be much more fragile. They are more easily refuted by empiric evidence or changing public moral standards. This happens without posing a threat to parties, because parties will be less dependent on these models. Consider a single-issue party that wants to defend the rights of workers: it is quite irrelevant whether the Marxist theory of capital is right or wrong. But for the Communist Party, this theory is the very essence of the party and cannot be conceived of as wrong. The reduced dependency of inclusive parties on single theories will allow us to more easily adapt to better models, much like the scientific method.

Do we need Big Pictures and ideologies to improve our society? Science did not advance via big, holistic theories[34]. Economies do not thrive on the search for ideal economic systems. Evolution is not propelled by the search for the perfect organism. Should we search for one big political solution instead of looking for many realistic, small solutions? I think not.

34 By which I mean theories that encompass everything, in contrast to specific aspects.

9 REPRESENTATION BY POLITICAL PARTIES

It can be said that representatives make choices for those they represent, in both politics and economics. One advantage of a representative system is that more specialized representatives can make better choices. For example, during an operation, a doctor can make lifesaving decisions while a patient is unconscious. To guarantee freedom of choice, a wide variety of choices must be available, including different options for one problem. But it is also important to have different independent options for different problems. As an example, someone might prefer Samsung to manufacture their mobile phone, while they prefer Apple to make their computer. Therefore, our political freedom is not sufficiently guaranteed if one can only be represented by one party at a time. Political freedom can only be assured when there is an independent choice between multiple representatives to solve different problems.

This proposal has an obvious criticism: if two representatives are chosen based on two different opinions, contradicting representation can occur. For example, you voted for both nature preservation and agricultural interests. These contradictions are common and require a case-by-case evaluation of the concerning laws. By aggregating the relevant case information, we (and our representatives) can decide what is best for specific situations. In economic cases, we might choose to buy milk and meat from two neighboring farmers. Therefore, these two farmers represent you in the making of milk and meat (the farming methods you support). If both farmers want to buy the same land to produce more, then conflicting interests emerge. The economic conflict of these farmers (representatives) will be solved by market mechanisms—which farmer makes the most money or which method of farming is more land dependent—and this process will result in one farmer buying the land. Whether this was the best outcome cannot be predicted. unavoidably, mistakes will be made—one farmer could overvalue the land and pay more than its value for his business. In order to keep the size of mistakes small, this optimization process is best done in a bottom-up free market. In a bottom-up free market, many small and independent decisions are made. In contrast, decisions are more dependent on each other in a top-down market, leading to larger, combined mistakes.

Even if one votes for parties that seem to explicitly contradict one another, there are still good reasons to do so. Consider a country with a large illegal immigrant population. Illegal immigrants might not be able to legally work or to let their children attend school; therefore, it is harder for them to integrate. A typical "left" solution would be the legalization of these illegal immigrants, while a typical "right" solution would be the deportation of these people. A citizen could vote for either the left or the right solution (via support for a representative), but it could also be reasonable to vote for both of them if one thinks that the status quo is the worst outcome.

10 POLITICAL CLEAVAGE

Political cleavages are problems that divide a population based on how citizens think they should be solved. These cleavages can align with parties (reinforcing cleavages) or within parties (crosscutting cleavage). Reinforcing cleavages should result in open discussions between advocates and adversaries as they work to find good solutions. However, because these open discussions occur between groups, they will create some polarization. In contrast, crosscutting cleavages will repress open discussion. Since the party can only be harmed by division within, an internal taboo or forced compromise is the preferred option. This might cause the problem to fester because it is not being solved, causing large and unexpected social disruptions.

Ostrogorski observed such an example in the middle of the nineteenth century, when the United States encountered an enormous problem that contributed to the end of the Whig Party and the emergence of the Republican Party. That problem was slavery. Ostrogorski wrote about the Democrats:

> While also divided on the question of the extension of slavery, the Democratic party preserved an appearance of unity and cohesion, thanks to the discipline and to the concessions which it was continually making to the slaveholders, under the influence of its Organization ... But these successive concessions, being of little use to the slaveholders, who were overrun by the development of free labour in the new Territories and unnerved by the growing opposition of public opinion in the free States, the flexibility of which, great as it was, had its limits, the alliance between slaveholders and the Democrats could not last. The party Organization resorted to all manner of manœuvres and expedients to maintain it ... The split that was brewing during the whole of Buchanan's Presidency, which was filled with struggles between the administration devoted to irreconcilable slaveholders and the northern Democrats, came to a head at the national convention of the party, which met at 1860, at Charleston ... The semblance of union in the party disappeared; the long struggle between the ambiguous situation

> kept up by the Organization and the naked truth of the slaveholders' aspirations was at an end ... Freed from the trammels with which these organizations had enveloped them, the principle of liberty on the one side and that of slavocracy on the other could stand up, meet face to face, and fight it out. But the conflict could no longer be settled in a peaceful way; it was too late for that ... [The] slavery conflict was left to the arbitrament of blood and iron.[35]

Suppressing discussion is the same method dictators use to stifle freedom in the name of stability. However, this promised stability is a fragile stability, susceptible at any time able to disruption by a large shock.[36] Institutions (NGOs, Parliament, media, etc.) must facilitate conflict resolution before a problem grows too large to be solved. Contemporary examples can be found in discussions of integration or minority rights (e.g. in Belgium: headscarf, animal slaughter without anesthesia).[37] The political fragility resulting from the exclusive party system should be considered the real cause of the American Civil War, while the conflict on slavery was the trigger.

Lipset, in contrast, argues that overlapping bases of cleavage contribute to the stability of democratic systems; that is, he prefers crosscutting cleavages over reinforcing cleavages.[38] Party cleavages therefore form a "catch-22."[39] Reinforcing cleavages facilitate open discussion of social

---

35 Ostrogorski, 1902, Vol II, p. 108-111.

36 Taleb and Blyth, 2011.

37 Both debates relate to the extent to which religious rights apply. The first to the wearing of head/face-covering clothing and the second to the religious slaughter of animals.

38 Abridged Ostrogorski and Lipset, 1982, Vol II, p. lxi.

39 A catch-22 is a paradoxical situation from which an individual cannot escape because of contradictory rules; e.g.: "How am I supposed to gain

problems. This creates some short-term instability in order to achieve long-term stability. Short-term instability can be absorbed by a stable society; this is accomplished by crosscutting cleavages, which group people with different opinions together. In an exclusive system, cleavages cannot be crosscutting and reinforcing at the same time. However, cleavages can be both crosscutting and reinforcing in an inclusive system, where citizens can cooperate in one party while opposing each other in other parties. The catch-22 is thus solved by inclusive parties.

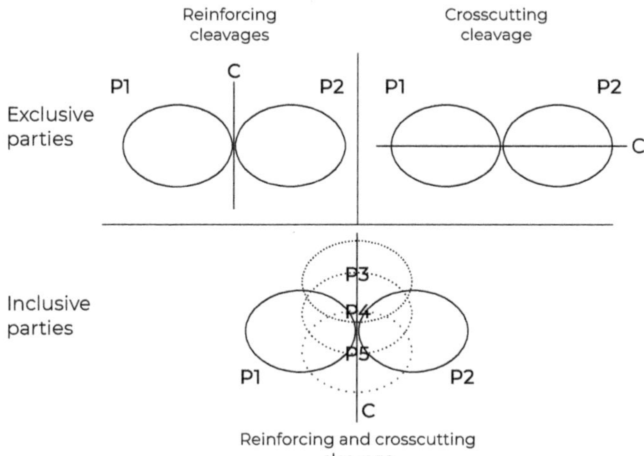

FIGURE 2.4: Schematic representation of the catch-22 of party cleavages. For the exclusive party system, cleavages can be reinforcing or crosscutting, but not both. For an inclusive party system, they can be both, thereby creating groups with political diversity; this is needed for short-term stability, while still allowing open discussions about social problems and creating long-term stability. Parties (**P1...P5**) and cleavage (**C**).

experience to find a good job if I'm constantly turned down for not having any experience?" See en.wikipedia.org/wiki/Catch-22_(logic)

11 INTRINSIC TRANSPARENCY

Some years ago I was having a chat with my former master thesis promoter at a PhD defense. Savvas Savvides is a Cypriot, and because he studied abroad he was unable to vote in elections until very recently. Because he wanted to educate himself before voting, he used a voting advice application (VAA). These web programs ask a series of questions and then, based on your answers, provide voting advice. VAAs are gaining popularity. According to Wikipedia, fifteen of twenty-two European countries had at least one VAA in 2007[40]. Some of the most successful programs were the Dutch Stemwijzer, with 4.7 million consultations in 2006 (40 percent of the electorate) and the German Wahl-O-Mat, with 6.7 million consultations in 2009 (12 percent of the electorate).

Being more informed is a good thing, so these programs must also be good, right? Not necessarily, because these programs are made by a person, and that person can influence the advice received by the program, therefore influencing voting behavior. Although experts might strive for neutral standards, VAAs remain a fragile tool that can mislead voters intentionally or by mistake. For example, VAAs often exclude parties based on arbitrary rules, such as a party being too small.[41] It might be harder for small parties to become more widely known if potential supporters rely on VAAs.

But why are these VAAs being used in the first place? Voting is essentially a questionnaire that you answer to

40 en.wikipedia.org/wiki/Voting_advice_application

41 https://web.archive.org/web/20190424202554/http://www.educatievestemtest.be/#faq-3

indicate which party or candidate you prefer. So voting advice applications are essentially questionnaires that help you with filling out another questionnaire. This is similar to having a manual that requires another manual to understand the first manual! Figure 2.5, based on XKCD's cartoon, helps visualize this.[42] I think it is clear that the first questionnaire (the voting ballot) is a poorly made questionnaire. Why is that? The exclusivity rule forces parties to have an opinion on all issues. This makes it impossible for all but the most informed citizens to compare these general parties. Voters react by either ignoring most of the programs or reducing them to the subject they find most important at the time.[43]. This somewhat explains the great success of politicians who simplify complex problems into one problem—a troublesome state for a system that assumes electors weigh their choices based on all problems. The voter could also ignore the programs and choose an appealing candidate, rendering the party's platform useless. Once again, inclusive, one-issue parties can solve these problems. Although there would be many more parties, it would be much easier for voters to decide which parties are relevant. The complexity of political decision-making is more transparent with many inclusive parties; this complexity is hidden when there are a few general, exclusive parties.

42 See xkcd.com/1343/

43 This is also a good explanation for floating voters Although these voters' opinions are largely unchanged, their priorities, and the parties they vote for, change from election to election.

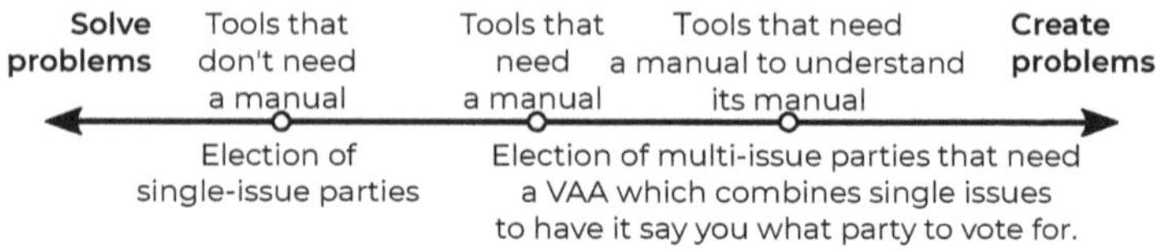

FIGURE 2.5: Tools are considered ineffective if they have a manual that requires another manual to understand them. Election systems based on exclusive parties are good examples of this, because they require another questionnaire (i.e., VAAs) for citizens to determine how to vote.

When political parties, and the choices they represent, become more transparent, people will be more willing to participate in the political system by voting and actively participating in these one-issue inclusive parties. In the eloquent words of Ostrogorski:

> By joining one of the parties which will be formed on this occasion, he will know exactly what he wants, what is the issue, to what he gives his adhesion, where he is going and how far he will go. The aim of the association being circumscribed, he will be able to follow the efforts made to realize it; his attention, no longer distracted by the multiplicity of objects with which a party burdens itself under the present system, will be concentrated, and will not weary so quickly. New problems will appeal to him, new parties will be formed to solve them, and he will have to decide what attitude he should take up with regard to them. He will be forced to examine his conscience oftener than he does now. The appeal addressed to the elector by the respective organizations on behalf of the cause which they represent will be heard far more effectively than under the present regime: confronted with a single well-defined question, the elector will be able to understand what is said to him, whereas now he is not.

> Those who have conducted election campaigns among the masses are unanimous on this point, they all agree that it is impossible to make the electors understand more than one question at a time, but that, on the other hand, if one deals with a single problem and takes trouble---one must take a great deal--to explain it well, one can drive it into the popular mind.[44] ... the limited nature of the pledges given by the citizen will keep alive his independence of mind like a fire which it will not let die out. With whatever combination he connects himself, he will always be able to differ from his associates on all points other than those which have brought them together.[45]

It is easier to form a party in an inclusive system. This will also improve transparency. Because of the high threshold to become a party and be to active in Parliament these days, non-party political organizations lobby the few present parties to enact change. Lobbying presents a greater advantage for organizations that work top-down. Because the popular opinion is less likely to benefit from top-down interests, lobbyists for those top-down organizations often prefer secrecy. In contrast, organizations that work bottom-up require support from the population, so they cannot work in secret. This makes it more difficult for bottom-up organizations to enact change, because they cannot refute the secret arguments of top-down organizations. Inclusive parties will make lobbying redundant: political organizations that require lobbying will themselves become parties, and they will then be able to directly affect policy. Because this direct action cannot be secret, it will level the playing field for both top-down and bottom-

44 I think this is applicable to all people, not just "the popular mind."

45 Ostrogorski, 1902, Part II, p659-661.

up organizations. I will discus this in greater detail in Chapter 3.

A third potential improvement in transparency can be found in political decision-making by traditionally marginalized groups in the exclusive party system. For example, migrant communities and their problems are often underrepresented in parliament. They face a dilemma: either join an existing party, with its associated priorities, in which they will be a minority, or create their own party that prioritizes their problems, in which they will be a majority. However, the latter solution will isolate them from other parties in the exclusive system, increasing their risk of becoming politically segregated and therefore politically irrelevant. In contrast, if these migrants could associate with an inclusive party, such as one constructed by these migrant communities, they could still participate in additional inclusive parties based on their personal preferences, which are unrelated to migration; this would improve their integration into the local society. Their own inclusive party would become a gateway for further participation in society. Then problems facing these groups, previously invisible to policy makers, would become more visible because they would have representative policymakers.

12 HYPERDEMOCRACY

Variation is essential in the creation of an anti-fragile political system. This is obvious: when there are more potential solutions, there is a greater chance of a good outcome. Greater diversity is achieved by more possibilities—both single solutions and combinations of these single solutions into composite solutions. For example, the iPhone was not revolutionary because of a single, novel feature; the new combination of features into one device was novel.

As explained earlier, the exclusive system, together with its consequential preference of ideologies, links one solution to another, hindering the formation of new combinations. The same problem has been encountered by biological life. Variations in the genetic information of organisms are carried from one generation to the next. But until about one billion years ago there was no simple way to combine variations in individual organisms to form new combinations. Evolution was dramatically propelled by the introduction of sexual reproduction. Instead of simply passing genetic information to the next generation—from one individual to another—genetic information from two individuals is mixed and then passed on to the next generation. This creates a system in which almost all variations in the genome are independent of each other over time.

A good name for a democratic system that uses an inclusive party system might be "hyperdemocracy." The prefix *hyper* comes from Greek, where it means "over" or "above." However, it has a more specific use in mathematics, where it refers to an object in the higher dimensions. For example, the cube is a three-dimensional object, while higher-dimension analogues are hypercubes. Another example is hypertext, the text within hyperlinks— an essential component of the World Wide Web, allowing us to surf from one page to another. Here, *hyper* refers to an added dimension that allows the user access to additional information that is contained in a one-dimensional sequence of regular text.

In physics, dimensions are independent directions. Regardless of forward or backward movement, you will never emerge above or below or to the left or to the right. In politics, we could view dimensions as the independent political choices we make. Because the party exclusivity rule prevents members from associating with other parties (by vote, participation, etc.), an exclusive party system is one dimensional. In an inclusive system, however, you can be linked to multiple parties at the same time, facilitating multidimensional choices.

By default, humans are multidimensional. Our genetics, environment, culture, and the people that surround us create many independent preferences. However, artificial separation created by the exclusivity rule projects these multidimensional political choices onto a single dimension. This fundamentally reshapes people's perceptions of others: for a person that identifies as "left," solutions given by the "right" become incomprehensible, and vice versa. This is exacerbated when the exclusivity of political parties is also combined with other exclusive characteristics, such as religion, nationality, or ethnicity.[46]

Multidimensionality also increases the level of democracy. Consider that the level of democracy represents the distribution of power. If one dictator holds all power, then this is the least democratic situation (lowest level). In contrast, a situation in which power is evenly distributed to all members of society is the most democratic situa-

46 Note that not all religions, nationalities, or ethnicities are exclusive. For example, polytheistic religions (e.g., the Romans were willing to accept the Greek and Egyptian gods) are considered to be more tolerant to other religions (Taleb, 2018). In addition, identities composed of multiple nationalities and ethnicities allow for inclusiveness.

tion (highest level). In a simplified exclusive system, there is one majority and one minority (one dimensional); therefore, the majority has power and the minority lacks power. In an inclusive system, however, there are multiple independent majorities and minorities. So, the identities of the majority and minority could vary with different decisions. Therefore, power will be much more evenly distributed between the people. This example illustrates how increasing dimensionality facilitates a more democratic system than currently available. Of course, for a representative democracy, people's representatives also need to think and vote independently; otherwise, the dimensionality of our society is again reduced to the number of independent groups (parties) in parliament. More on this in Chapter 3.

13 THE EXCLUSIVE PARTY SYSTEM ENABLES TOTALITARIANISM

While the exclusive party system is defined as being exclusive to individuals, totalitarian parties are a subset of these parties that seek to extend exclusivity to the whole nation. While exclusive parties have to extend their scope to cover all political issues, totalitarian parties seek to extend their power beyond politics, into the judiciary system, media, religion, economy, etc. They will disband or absorb competing parties and most organizations of civil society because these groups always pose a risk to the power of the totalitarian party.

Several already-discussed factors that are inherent to the exclusive party system can facilitate the rise of a totalitarian party. For example, ideology and political segregation facilitates the vilification of others. The exclusive system forces parties to extend their programs to all issues, benefiting large parties. These large parties are more effective in political segregation, and they also have an advantage in achieving totalitarianism because, once in power, they can take control of state apparatuses much more easily than small, single-issue parties.

Luckily for us, just as most pre-cancerous cells never become cancer, most exclusive parties never become totalitarian. But any party must become exclusive before it can become totalitarian. I believe that without the exclusivity rule, the Nazi and communist parties would not have been able to seize power and create such suffering for millions of people in the 20th century.

14 SUMMARY

I began this chapter by looking for a solution to create necessary political decentralization. As illustrated in the previous chapter, this is important for improving our political system and also, indirectly, for decentralizing the economy. The solution proposed in this chapter is to convert our exclusive party system into an inclusive one. This will allow citizens to vote, associate, and participate concurrently with multiple parties. However, I also illustrated that the conversion of exclusive parties to inclusive parties has many benefits beyond decentralization. Party inclusivity—that is, the absence of party exclusivity—will improve democracy by increasing political freedom and flexibility; reducing political polarization; increasing participation, intrinsic transparency, political innovation, and specialization; and reducing the risks of negative political Black Swans (e.g., the rise of a dictator or a civil war).

CHAPTER 3

REPRESENTATION

1 A NEW PARLIAMENT

The legislative branch, examples of which are the British Parliament, the German Bundestag, and the US Congress, is certainly the institution that best embodies contemporary representative democracy. Trust in representative democracy therefore stands or falls with citizens' trust in their legislative branch and its representatives. In the United States, Congress has become a deeply distrusted institution. In Belgium, the Federal Parliament more often resembles a theater in which the representatives have to abide by the commands of the exclusive parties. Although there is a theoretical constitutional distinction between the executive and legislative powers, most laws (greater than 90 percent) are proposed by the government, not parliament.[1] As I argued in Chapter 2, the participation of more specialized, inclusive parties will facilitate greater independence for parliaments because they are less dependent on external specialists from NGOs or corporations.

In the previous chapter, I outlined the detrimental effects of exclusive parties, focusing on the harm caused when there are few viable political parties. Increasing the number of viable political parties can be accomplished by lowering the threshold for new parties. However, the ex-

1 Huyse, 2014.

clusivity of political parties is not the only restriction we need to lift in order to increase the number of viable political parties. We also need to increase the number of representatives that can act on behalf of these numerous parties.

The first requirement for this new parliament is for it to be much less restrictive on the number of political parties participating at any given time. Currently, the theoretical maximum number of parties that can be represented in an exclusive party system is the number of elected representatives. But in practice, it ranges from one (e.g., China) to about a dozen. For the new parliament, I envision as many as hundreds of political parties to be represented. Since these parties will be one-issue parties, they do not need to be represented in discussions of every issue in parliament. Only when an issue relevant to a party is discussed, that party should be represented. Because the legislative power is composed of representatives, changing how the legislative power works can be achieved by changing *how* and *whom* the representatives represent.

2 TWO MODELS OF REPRESENTATION

A good start to the discussion of how and whom a member of parliament should represent constituents began on the 3rd of November, 1774. On that day, after being elected, British philosopher Edmund Burke made the following statement:

> Parliament is not a congress of ambassadors from different and hostile interests; which interests each must maintain, as an agent and advocate, against other agents and advocates; but parliament is a deliberative assembly of one nation, with one interest, that of the whole;

> where, not local purposes, not local prejudices, ought to guide, but the general good, resulting from the general reason of the whole. You choose a member indeed; but when you have chosen him, he is not member of Bristol, but he is a member of parliament. If the local constituent should have an interest, or should form an hasty opinion, evidently opposite to the real good of the rest of the community, the member for that place ought to be as far, as any other, from any endeavor to give it effect.[2]

With this quote, Edmund Burke characterized both how and for whom the parliamentary representative should represent. First *how*: parliamentary representatives think for themselves—in other words, they act independently. This is also known as the trustee model of representation. Independence is widely acknowledged as a fundamental condition for obtaining more accurate estimates by aggregating information. This holds for data, models, and also opinions. For example, a scientist that copies data to obtain "more data" is a fraud—the "new" data is completely dependent on previous data and therefore has no added value. Translating this analogy to real-life scenarios in which people view opinions as data, the need for independence is also required for the wisdom of the crowds.[3] In his book named after this phenomenon, Surowiecki explains the necessary conditions for a crowd to make more accurate conclusions than the single smartest person in the group. The essential conditions for wisdom of the crowds, according to Surowiecki, are diversity of opinion, independence, decentralization, and a form of information aggregation. The book also illustrates what happens when those conditions

2 Burke, 1774.
3 Surowiecki, 2004.

are not met and the crowd fails in making a good judgment.

Surowiecki argues that any opinion has both an information component and an error component. When combining dependent opinions, the errors will align and the resulting outcome will be biased. In contrast, if opinions are independent, the errors will cancel out and the aggregated opinions will reach more accurate conclusions. Transferring this analogy to the case of a parliamentary representative, the official who simply copies another representative's opinion without forming an opinion of their own does not add any value. We should not tolerate this fraud in a democracy.

Because parties currently require representatives to be dependent on the party, these parties weaken the ability of a parliament to act as a wise crowd. Thinking independently is important for a representative to criticize faulty laws; each of them have some personal knowledge that others lack. Hence, we should liberate representatives from the subjugation of political parties. In contrast to the trustee model, we have the delegate model: the representative only follows the guidelines of their constituents, acting dependently. The advantage of the trustee model lies in the ability of the representative to best pass information from those they represent to the body of which they are a member. This does become more difficult when there is significant variation in the opinions of those that are represented.

Our second consideration is *for whom*. According to Burke, the parliamentary representative should pursue the interests of the whole community (that is, the greater good), instead of only the interests of a specific group. The ideal—that representatives strive for the greater good—is commonly accepted by many. For example, the Belgian constitution states in article 42: *"De leden van beide Kamers vertegenwoordigen de Natie en niet enkel degenen die hen hebben verkozen"*—"The members of both chambers represent the nation and not only their own electors."

Although how and whom a representative represents are two different questions, they are nonetheless linked. To represent a large, heterogeneous group, the representative must independently compile information, and constituent interests must be balanced to reach an overall beneficial solution. In contrast, when representing a smaller, more homogeneous group, they can strictly follow instructions, without needing to look for a balanced solution themselves. This theory is supported by a study that evaluated representatives' self-identified role as a trustee or delegate. Trustees were defined as those who worked independently, while delegates were those who worked dependently. Self-identified trustees were proportionally more state-oriented (larger, hence more variation), while self-identified delegates were more district-oriented (smaller, hence less variation).[4]

However, the Burkean representative ideal seems impossible in the current reality: representatives mostly pursue the interests of their electoral supporters or, more directly, those of their political party and the elites that influence parties. Some classic political pluralists justify this by assuming that the combination of advocates of specific interests can form a democratic equilibrium, in which there is a balance between different interests. This seems very

4 Eulau et al., 1959.

implausible to me. If we imagine a court of law where justice is only spoken by advocates of specific interests, then "justice" would very soon become the law of the strong: those with the most advocates would claim justice.

Given these arguments, it might seem ideal to only be represented by those striving for the common good. However, this model lacks diversity and opposition. Antifragile systems need generators of variability to create opportunities and flaws, from which we learn to adapt to new conditions (See Chapter 1). Just as a court of law without judges would not serve justice, neither would a court of law without advocates serve justice. So I suggest that we do not limit ourselves to only one representative model; both types of representation should be present in parliament. However, as they are intrinsically in conflict, different people should be represented by these two types. This would enable the combination of both models while safeguarding citizens from conflicts of interest. These two types of representatives are the party's representatives, who act for a specific interest by the delegate model, and the people's representatives, who act for the general interest by the trustee model.

3 PEOPLE'S AND PARTY REPRESENTATIVES

In an ideal world, parliament would be a place of public debate where reasonable humans try to persuade each other what is best for the common good. However, as it is currently run by interest group advocates, persuasion of one representative to another cause has little use. Consider this example of how the chamber generally runs: the majority of members are familiar with a given proposal and vote with a well-known deafness to criticism. The minority is already convinced of the awfulness of the proposal. Since political fractions have already formed, representatives put less effort into the lawmaking procedure—why make much effort if you are already sure it will pass the vote? As advocates and critics cannot persuade additional representatives, they lapse into rhetoric performances to signal their efforts for "the good cause" to their partisan supporters.

In a court of law, different parties present their views of the facts and important interpretations of the law surrounding these facts. They do this to obtain justice, by influencing a specific verdict based on the party's case. These parties are often represented by professional advocates: lawyers. Judges then make a decision based on the law and the presented facts. For some very important cases, a group of judges makes decisions to reduce the impact of random interpretations of an individual judge.

By combining the principles of the current court of law with the parliament, I suggest the introduction of two distinct parliamentarians that relate to each other like judges and advocates: people's representatives and party representatives. Party representatives will advocate for specific interests and propose new laws (proposal power). People's representatives will hear different viewpoints and identify a consensus that benefits the common good and then decide between the law propositions, based on the presented facts (voting power). Basically, the party representatives would propose laws and the people's representatives would vote on law propositions. In this setting, the people's representatives would be present for the proposal of each law, but only the parties relevant to the proposed law would be present for the necessary procedures (discussion, presenting evidence, and actual voting) on the proposed law.

The separation of legislative power into proposing and voting blocks should enable real discussion. The party's representatives will be obligated to persuade independent people's representatives of the benefits of their law proposals. The independence of the people's representatives should be ensured by including many parties in parliament; this should also limit the power of each individual party. Additionally, a distinct voting method for the people's representatives will enhance their dependence on the complete electorate, rather than on partisans with specific interests (see Section5). Since the votes of the majority of the people's representatives in parliament will become more uncertain, greater efforts will be made to construct good laws. Any flaw in the proposal might cause it to be rejected by the people's representatives, even if the spirit of the law is well intended.

Before modern political parties were needed to win elections, there were alliances in parliamentarian assemblies. For example, the Whigs and Tories were political factions in seventeenth to nineteenth century England, before they transformed into parties that organized to win elections. These associations were partially based on the mutual interests of members: if you support my proposal, I will support yours.[5] This has certainly deteriorated the independence of representatives. In my proposed system, proposals and votes are required from different members of parliament (people's and party representatives); therefore this bargaining cannot be directly accomplished.[6] Therefore, this is an additional safeguard to maintain the independence of people's representatives.

Although people's and party representatives should mostly be independent of each other, they will still be able to influence each other. People's representatives will be able to criticize and reject party representatives' proposals. Party representatives can likewise influence via their law proposals or criticize the choices of the people's representatives. Additionally, both types of representatives can provide voting advice to the public, based on the legislative history of party and people's representatives.

The separation between proposing and voting on laws has been partially observed in the European Union (EU). Unfortunately, the implementation has been poor, resulting in the creation of an elite, bureaucratic, opaque, and generally anti-democratic institution.[7] Instead of enabling

5 While modern party alliances function differently, bargaining with votes is still done by modern parties. Parties even assign specialized members (whip or faction leader) in order to maintain loyal voting behavior.

6 Indirect bargaining to influence people's representatives outside of parliament (lobbying) would also be much harder because it would be criminalized; see Section 9

7 For example, in 2015, the EU commission received the results of a study for which it had paid €360,000. This study contained conclusions that undermine the need for stronger copyright protection, an unfavorable

many specialized parties to propose legislature and then allowing representatives to filter the bad propositions, only the European Commission, a small group of elite lawmakers, has the power to propose laws.[8] This bottleneck creates an opening for lobbyists to influence proposals in their favor, limiting the influence of individual citizens.

In this new model, people's representatives would be elected individually while party representatives would be chosen by the parties that were elected as organizations. It is important for people's representatives to be individually elected. They have the final responsibility on new laws; therefore, they need to be held responsible for their actions, both by electoral means or, in case of criminal wrongdoing, by effective criminal sanctioning. For a natural person, punishments, such as restrictions of freedom, are more severe and less avoidable than those applied to legal persons like organizations. In contrast, organizations are ideal catalysts of change and can create support for specific social needs. Given the party's function, it would not make sense to directly elect party representatives because this could create a situation in which the directly elected party representative has excessive power over the party that they represent. Instead, when the party is elected, they choose one (or even more) delegates who can act as a party representative. This enables flexibility for the party to make, defend, and criticize law proposals however they see fit. Sanctioning parties is more complex and,

conclusion for corporate copyright lobbyists. The commission failed to make this study public until it was actively requested by MEP Julia Reda of the Pirate Party in mid 2017. juliareda.eu/2017/09/secret-copyright-infringement-study/

8 en.wikipedia.org/wiki/European_Union_legislative_procedure#Commission

perhaps, undesirable, as can be seen in the example of *Vlaams Blok*, a far-right Belgian political party. In 2004, the Court of Appeal in Ghent ruled that some of the party's organizations had breached the 1981 anti-racism law, and the party was sanctioned for discrimination.[9] Although the party was dissolved because of this conviction, a new party, the *Vlaams Belang*, was immediately created by the former members of the *Vlaams Blok*.

This new system of a parliament, with people's and party representatives, is analogous to the system of courthouses, which work with judges and lawyers. The largest difference is that making a law requires general rules based on the specific needs of people, while applying the law implies a specific ruling from general rules. Lawyers and party representatives provide variation in viewpoints. Judges and people's representatives select theories from the given variation that can be applied to either a specific or the general case.

Table 3.1: Comparison of People's and Party representatives

People's Representatives	Party Representatives
Generalist	Specialist
Defend general interest	Defend specific interest
Trustee (Burkean) model	Delegate model
Diversity of majorities	Diversity of all
Vote on/criticize law proposals	Make/defend/criticize law proposals
Elect person	Elect party
Elect to accept/reject	Elect to prioritize
Symmetric voting	Positive asymmetric voting
Low dependency on popularity	High dependency on popularity

9 en.wikipedia.org/wiki/Vlaams_Blok

4 COMPLETE CHOICE VOTING

Voting is regarded by many as a cornerstone of democracy. I think voting can be related to democracy as statistics is related to science: indispensable, but often misused. Let me start to illustrate this with the absurd but horrifying tale of Fritz, a fictitious Nazi officer at a concentration camp. Although he is a Nazi, he feels that he should legitimize some of his actions by the vote of his entire camp. The camp mainly includes prisoners, but there is also a minority of well-armed soldiers. So he decides to let his camp vote on whether (a) they should kill all the prisoners or (b) torture and then kill them. The voting day proceeds: all of the prisoners refuse to vote, because they think that voting legitimizes the choices. Almost all of the soldiers, in contrast, vote to kill the prisoners, as torturing takes too much effort for them anyway. Fritz is happy because he has a clear majority that legitimizes his action to kill the prisoners.

This story illustrates how the act of voting does not always legitimize the results of the vote. Moreover, if no real choice is being given to the people, they will abandon participation in the vote. You might argue that this story is too far-fetched and could never describe real life events. However, on March 16, 2014, the people of Crimea had a referendum with two choices: reunification with Russia or becoming an independent state within Ukraine. The result was the reunification of Crimea with Russia. To reject both of those choices was not an option.[10] A second example is the 2016 presidential election in the United States, primarily between Donald Trump and Hillary Clin-

10 en.wikipedia.org/wiki/Crimean_status_referendum,_2014#Choices

ton. While Donald Trump won, polls showed that Trump and Clinton were the two most unpopular candidates in thirty years.[11] In addition, voter turnout was the lowest in twenty years, giving the impression that people disliked the candidates and politics so much that they did not even bother to vote.[12] It is likely that there is an even larger group of US citizens that did not want either Trump or Clinton as their president.

A more subtle example is the French presidential election system. If no candidate can obtain a majority in the first round, a run-off election is held between the candidates with the highest number of votes. This system attempts to guarantee the support of a majority of voters for the winning candidate. Unfortunately, it is unsuccessful; by reducing the options for the electorate down to two candidates, a mathematical majority is always guaranteed. However, this is a fake majority, because voters did not have sufficient choices. Consider the made-up country Unanimistan, the most democratic country in the universe, where all decisions are made by unanimous run-off elections. These elections would proceed as follows: if no candidate becomes the unanimous winner in the first round, a run-off will be performed with only the candidate with the highest vote—unanimity is ensured!

These real and fictitious examples demonstrate that voting is controlled by those who control the options at the ballot box. This allows elites to have power over voters, making voting a mere illusion of power. When the propositions are bad, there are no benefits to voting. How

11 www.usatoday.com/story/news/politics/onpolitics/2016/08/31/poll-clinton-trump-most-unfavorable-candidates-ever/89644296/

12 edition.cnn.com/2016/11/11/politics/popular-vote-turnout-2016/

can we counter this? I suggest the use of complete choice voting, which means that the voter should always be able to vote on all possible options. This may sound impossible, with infinite possibilities to choose from. But options can be grouped: when I do not want a rabbit for my birthday, I also know that I do not want a white, black, or brown rabbit. This means that we can have complete choice for all questions by giving two answers for each question "Do you want A?" "Yes, I want A," and "No, I don't want A." The latter choice is an affirmative choice for all options that do not include A. The completeness of choices A and NOT A is analogous to the sum of the probability space being one.[13] Complete choice voting can thus be viewed as a similar process to the scientific tests of hypotheses. By voting, we test whether a majority supports option A over option NOT A. If A is accepted, we jointly chose A. If NOT A is selected, we maintain the status quo. However, this does not mean that we want the status quo—there might be unknown options that are more favorable. Yet, for us to chose any of these additional options, we need to vote again. Any vote in which we cannot reject the propositions should be considered undemocratic, similar to theories that cannot be falsified are unscientific.

The majority rule has been used to vote on the acceptance or rejection of a particular law proposal. We should expand this beyond voting on laws (which are applicable to all citizens) to the selection of people's representatives.[14] It seems fair that we should vote on, and thus control, those who represent all of us equally, as those who represent all

13 A probability space is a measure space such that the measure of the whole space is equal to one. See en.wikipedia.org/wiki/Probability_-space

14 Those who represent all people, not subsets of the population (parties)

of us vote on the laws that control all of us. When an employer selects a suitable applicant, they will first evaluate whether the applicants are suitable for the job; if they are, the secondary question of "which candidate is best" becomes relevant. Suppose you were in a plane that was about to take off. None of the candidates to fly the plane have successfully completed a pilot exam, but nonetheless the best candidate was selected. Would you feel safe boarding this plane to fly home? Probably not. Most classical political scientists working on voting theory seem to relish finding the best candidate while ignoring whether the representatives are actually suitable for the job. If we apply this logic to regular jobs, why are we not applying these standards to the most important political positions? This is like asking which homeopathic medicine best cures cancer (hint: they are all equally good). If all candidates are unsuitable (e.g., Hillary Clinton & Donald Trump), none should be elected.[15] Therefore, it is wiser to elect the worst candidate who has greater approval than disapproval, than it is to elect the best candidate who people more strongly disapprove of than approve.

5 HOW YOU VOTE IS WHAT YOU GET

I have hopefully convinced you that we only need to measure the approval and disapproval of candidates. Therefore, a voting method should be easy to choose. The approval voting method allows each voter to approve as many candidates as desired. However, this method creates an asymmetry, because although the approval of a candidate gives us positive evidence of support for a candidate, the

15 www.usatoday.com/story/news/politics/onpolitics/2016/08/31/poll-clinton-trump-most-unfavorable-candidates-ever/89644296/

lack of approval is not negative evidence; rather, it is a lack of evidence. A voter could, for instance, not know the candidate or not be convinced that the candidate is ideal, without thinking of them as bad.[16] In contrast, disapproval voting generates evidence of disapproval but not of approval.[17] Therefore, these methods are asymmetric: the inverse result does not indicate evidence for the inverse attitude. Approval voting is best called a positive asymmetric method, because it can give evidence for a positive attitude; disapproval voting is similarly best called a negative asymmetric method. It is also possible to have a symmetric voting method. By allowing each voter to either explicitly approve or disapprove of a candidate, we can obtain evidence of both the positive and negative attitudes toward the candidates.

Why should we care whether a voting method is symmetric or asymmetric? Because people's representatives and parties' tasks, and those they aim to represent, are different; therefore, the selection method for voting them into office should also select and (dis)incentivize differently. A symmetric voting method is more suitable for electing people's representatives, while a positive asymmetric voting method would be better for electing parties.

16 Alcantud and Laruelle, 2014.

17 Human opinions are more complex than just being *for* or *against* something. Human opinions can also be *not for* and *not against* something because of uncertainty—i.e., neutral. To be *for* or *against* something requires an active choice. People prefer the default in decision making, which is also known as the default effect or status quo bias. (E. J. Johnson and Goldstein, 2004; S. Johnson and Zeckhauser, 2014) This has also been observed in voting, where people overly prefer "0" or another neutral vote. See rangevoting.org/RateScaleResearch.html. Simply said: for humans, action has the burden of proof.

Let us consider the people's representative. As they represent the whole electorate, we can assume that the more the electorate approves of the candidate, the better the representative. Indeed, in almost all voting systems, more favorable candidates have a higher probability of election. However, the most common voting systems, which are positive asymmetric, can reward polarizing candidates over favorable candidates.

Let us distinguish the three groups of voting systems by their options of voting: symmetric $\{-1, 0, +1\}$; asymmetric positive $\{0, +1\}$; and asymmetric negative $\{-1, 0\}$. Disapproving votes—$\{-1\}$—reduce the chance of being elected, approving votes—$\{+1\}$—increase the chance of being elected, and neutral votes—$\{0\}$—do not change the chance of being elected.

The more positive a random person's attitude toward a candidate, the more likely they will approve (and less likely they will disapprove) of that candidate. In short, better candidates will get more approving votes. However, the statement, "candidates with more approving votes are better candidates" is not necessarily true in a voting system that cannot distinguish disapproval from a neutral attitude toward a candidate (positive asymmetric). This can therefore be exploited by polarization. When the electorate has a polarized opinion of candidates, there will be more votes with positive and negative attitudes and fewer with a neutral attitude. But because a positive asymmetric voting method does not differentiate between negative and neutral attitudes, the only observed outcome for a more polarizing candidate is more approving votes. Therefore, a polarizing candidate is more likely to be elected.

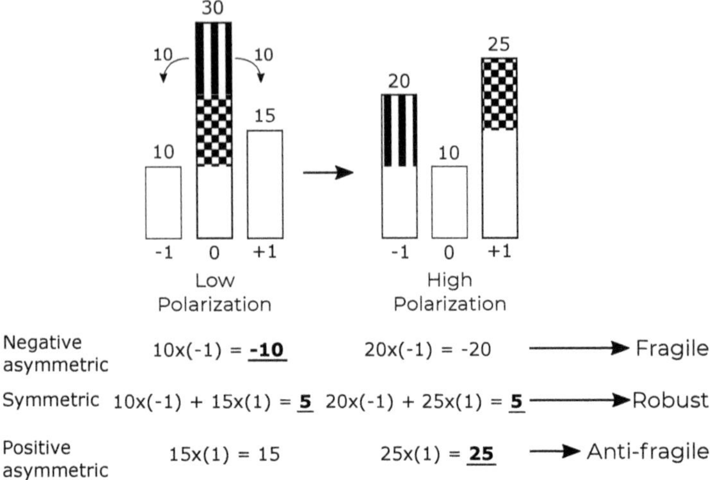

FIGURE 3.1: An illustration of the differences between negative asymmetric, symmetric, and positive asymmetric voting methods. The voting methods used here either add the negative votes, all votes, or only the positive votes. Higher scores result in a higher chance of being elected. Negative asymmetric voting is most successful with less polarization; positive asymmetric voting is most successful with more polarization; and symmetric voting is not affected by polarization.

In contrast, polarization leads to a disadvantage in negative asymmetric voting systems because no distinction is made between neutrality and disapproval. Polarization is a form of variation, and benefiting from variation means anti-fragility. Therefore, electable candidates are anti-fragile in positive asymmetric voting systems, while they are fragile in negative asymmetric voting systems and robust in symmetric voting systems. They are robust in symmetrical voting systems because polarization increases both disapproval and approval votes; therefore, there is no net result on the candidate's electoral outcome. Consequently, positive asymmetric voting methods will generate polarization; negative asymmetric voting methods will reduce it; and symmetric voting systems will have no influence on polarization.

Since we do not want people's representatives to gain advantages by polarization, we should either use a symmetric or negative asymmetric voting system. However, a negative asymmetric voting system could punish candidates too much for mistakes, which could have the unwanted effect of reduced transparency by candidates. For example, vocalizing a strong opinion on a subject that is controversial could polarize public opinion toward the candidate. Therefore, a negative voting system could create a strong incentive to self-censor these opinions and suppress an open debate. Hence, a symmetric voting method is preferable for people's representatives.

In contrast, variation is ideal for parties, because they should represent different points of view of our society; therefore, the positive asymmetric method is preferred for electing political parties. Increased variation requires increasing the approval of a subgroup in a party at the cost of increasing the disapproval of another subgroup for that same party. However, parties should act in the interests of the controlling subgroups; so the disapproval of other groups toward that party should not matter. The current positive asymmetric voting systems can polarize candidates via both selection and adaptation. Since polarizing the electorate generates higher numbers of votes, polarizing candidates are more likely to be selected again. But candidates might also adapt and then polarize voters with controversial points of view. For example, they could scapegoat a minority whose votes they do not seek. Groups that are less polarizing for any reason (culture, nature, etc.) will have a disadvantage in positive asymmetric voting systems. For example, suppose that men are more polarizing than women.[18] If this is true, women will be less likely to be elected in a positive asymmetric voting system than men, but not in a symmetric voting system, which is robust toward polarization.

As discussed in Chapter 2, economic actors can be described as economic representatives. For example, your baker is your representative in bread baking problems. Purchases are the voting system by which the buyers of products/services transfer power to the provider of these products/services.[19] Representatives with more money (votes) will become more powerful in the economic system, giving them more decision-making power for more and larger economic problems. Note that this voting system is positive asymmetric—one can only buy (vote) with positive money. This is reasonable, because economic representatives only represent their buyers—only those that buy bread from the baker should be affected by their decisions. This example is a contrast to politics: decisions become laws that apply to all voters, even those who did not vote for a representative.

18 While I did not find direct evidence for sex-dependent capability of polarization, there is some indirect evidence that supports it. Past meta-analyses have found that males, regardless of age, engaged in more physical and verbal aggression, while a small effect was observed for females engaging in more indirect aggression, such as rumor-spreading or gossiping. Additionally, women are generally more agreeable than men, which reduces women's ability to polarize.(Del Giudice, 2015) This might also explain the observed tendencies to patriarchal societies in history. Simple methods to show political power—e.g. the person that rallies the most people to the main square wins—are also a positive asymmetric voting method.

19 en.wikipedia.org/wiki/Dollar_voting

Therefore, an asymmetric voting system is compatible with economic decision-making, while a symmetric voting system is compulsory for political decision-making.[20]

6 POPULARITY

"Unknown, unloved" is an adage that seems to hold for many things, including elections. Elections are too often reduced to popularity contests in which rallying as many people as possible becomes the criterion for evaluating candidates, whatever the message. One problem with assuming that popular politicians are good politicians is that politicians become too dependent on the organizations that make them popular: political parties and the media. People's representatives should be independent of such influences; they should represent the interests of the citizens. Political parties have been so influential in the popularization of political candidates that some political theorists have defined political parties as organizations whose primary goal is to win elections.[21] For example, in the United States, the main purpose of both the Democratic National Committee (DNC) and Republican National Committee (RNC) is to facilitate the election of party members. The fragility induced by depending on these organizations was illustrated by the 2016 presidential election. First, the DNC was likely internally biased for Hillary Clinton and against Bernie Sanders. Second, DNC hacking might have negatively effected Clinton's ability to win the election. In an inclusive party system, parties will be more focused

20 This ignores the ability of the consumer to sue for damages, creating a form of negative voting and, therefore, creating some symmetry in the economic voting system.

21 e.g., rational-efficient perspective (Katz and Crotty, 2006, p. 9–10)

on content than candidates. Therefore, the decreased dependence of people's representatives on parties might also cause parties to be less dependent on specific persons.

The media has also been a major factor in the creation of politicians' popularity. One straightforward example is the application of state-governed propaganda to control the information that reaches the public. However, in a democracy, we should expect an independent power, the media, to be free from the influence of political elites. The candidates' strong need for popularity in current voting systems has prevented that independence. It is easy to see many strong ties between the political elite and the media: e.g., Rupert Murdoch–Tony Blair[22] and Steve Bannon–Donald Trump.[23] Even more worrisome are media elites that become politically powerful themselves, like Silvio Berlusconi in Italy.

The reciprocal dependency of media and politics can also lead to biased media. The most clear examples can be seen in the pillarized societies of early- and mid-twentieth century Belgium and the Netherlands. Most media organizations were explicitly linked to a political pillar, preventing citizens from creating independent opinions for themselves. Although some rejoice in the rise of social media at the expense of traditional media, there are still problems with independence. Although content creation in social media is definitely more decentralized, the distribution and prioritization might be more centralized. Google, Facebook, Twitter, and reddit, to name a few, create al-

22 Blair is the former UK prime minister and is godfather to Murdoch's daughter. Murdoch is the owner of 21st Century Fox and News Corp.

23 Bannon, former executive chair of Breitbart News, LLC, was appointed chief executive of Trump's 2016 presidential campaign.

gorithms that rank and sometimes censor (e.g., spam and fake news) on a massive scale. For some of these portals, it might not always be clear what is a highly ranked story or a paid advertisement, opening possibilities for voter manipulation (e.g., by sponsored trolls, Cambridge Analytica).

The need for popularity, and the subsequent dependence on parties and media, is caused by voting systems that have a linear reward for fame. Why should a system reward a people's representative for being well-known? If the candidate is unknown, then the number of votes a candidate receives might not be a good estimate of the people's opinion on that candidate. The more people know about a candidate, the more certain that the observed voting score reflects the voting score for a hypothetical case in which everyone knows the candidate.[24]

Using this reasoning, a well-known candidate should have an advantage over a less-known candidate at the ballot box. For example, it seems reasonable that Candidate A, with 2000 pro votes and 1000 contra votes, wins over Candidate B, who receives just 20 pro votes and 10 contra votes, even though both candidates have equal proportions of pro and contra votes. The voting score should reflect certainty. However, should this be linear? Returning to our example, if five more people vote for Candidate A, the score for Candidate A would barely change. In contrast, five additional people can significantly change the score for Candidate B. Therefore, it does not seem reasonable to have a linear reward for being well-known. An increase in a voting score as a result of being more known should be

24 In statistical terminology: a consistent parameter estimate converges to the parameter as the sample size increases.

greater when you are unknown than if you were well-known (i.e., concave payoff).

Let us compare two voting schemes: (1) the number of positive votes minus the number of negative votes ($N_p - N_n$), and (2) the ratio of positive votes and negative votes ($\frac{N_p}{N_n}$). If we compare these two voting schemes for a case in which three voters are for and two are against a candidate, and a case in which two hundred voters are for and three hundred are against, we observe some key differences. For scheme one, there is a much higher voting score when more people vote ($3 - 2 \ll 300 - 200$). In the second voting scheme, the same voting score is obtained, despite a different number of people voting ($\frac{2}{3} = \frac{200}{300}$). Therefore, a ratio-based voting method provides no advantage to popularity. This might be dangerous because it might favor unknown candidates too much; hence a voting method with a limited reward for popularity is needed (e.g., soft quorum range voting[25] or soft quorum majority voting; see Section 7). Soft quorum voting methods work by adding a fixed number of neutral votes (or an equal number of pro and contra-votes) to all candidates. Therefore, we create a prior baseline that will affect candidates who have insufficient votes. As candidates have more votes, their soft quorum score will move away from the prior baseline toward their true score. An example with candidates Alice and Bob is given in Figure 3.2.

While a voting system to elect parties should be considered decisive for the subgroup, it should only be suggestive for the whole of society. Since all suggestions from all citizens cannot realistically be evaluated, we should pri-

25 rangevoting.org/BetterQuorum.html

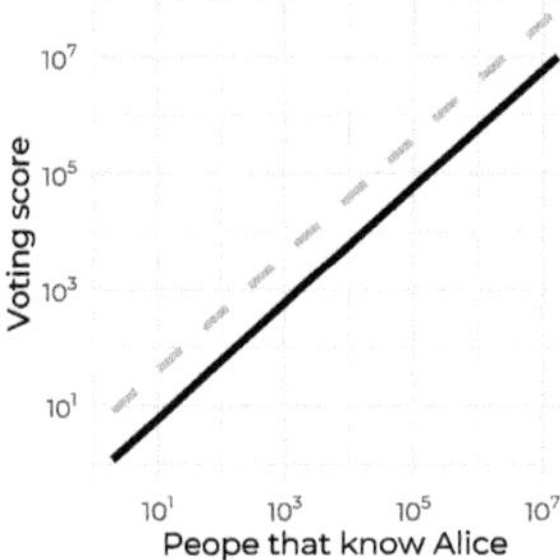

(a) In a voting system that is linearly affected by popularity, Bob will always win over Alice.

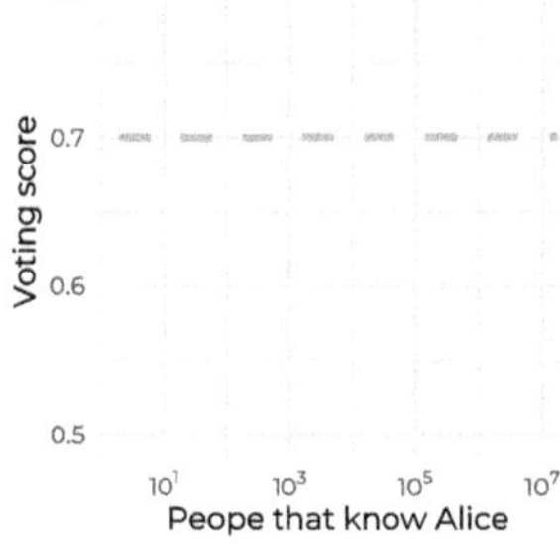

(b) This voting system, based on a ratio, is not affected by popularity; therefore, Alice always wins over Bob.

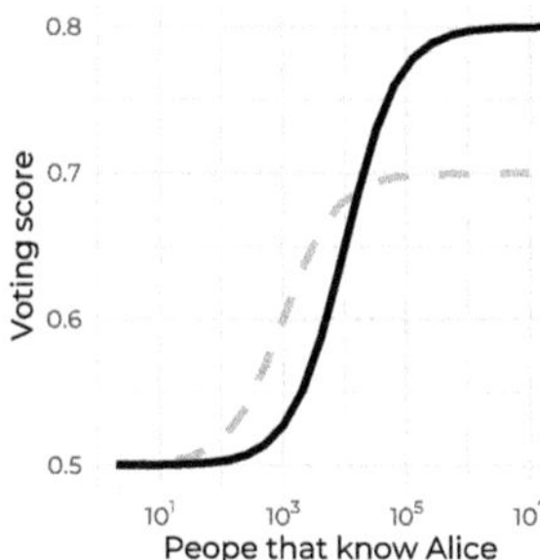

(c) In this quorum-based voting system, Bob will win when there are few people that know Bob and Alice. But as the popularity of both candidates increases, Alice will take the lead, even though she is less famous than Bob.

FIGURE 3.2: Three ways to account for popularity in a voting score. In this example Bob (dashed line) is always 10 times more popular than Alice (solid line), but Alice is 10 percent more suitable than Bob according to the people that know them. The third voting system (c) facilitates a good balance between requiring popularity to have some certainty, without having popularity become the most determining factor.

oritize evaluating those suggestions with greater support. As we have discussed, the decisive power that affects all citizens—voting on law proposals—is reserved for people's representatives. Furthermore, even if the voting system for parties depends on popularity, the consequences of additional votes will be capped. Parties that "win" the election can send a party's representative to parliament; however, because that representative could suggest the same number of law proposals as two other party representatives, party presence is more important than the number of representatives. Therefore, we will limit the number of representatives of a winning party to one. This will create a qualitative, rather than quantitative, party election.[26] Therefore, additional votes for parties do not result in more seats or more power for that party. Even if multiple seats are obtained by duplicate parties, their power would not significantly increase because they can only suggest laws, and the suggestion of multiple identical proposals will likely have a small effect on policy.

In short, the current voting systems overly reward popular candidates at the expense of qualified candidates. This creates a weakness for our democracy because candidates become overly dependent on institutions that increase their popularity: the media and political parties. The system proposed in this book would separately mediate this problem for different types of representation. The people's representatives require a voting method that balances the quality of a candidate (e.g., the ratio between pro and contra votes) with their popularity (the number of people that voted). For party representatives, the number of votes is very important: it should reflect the favor of the

26 This will reduce the zero-sum game characteristics between parties, as there is little to gain from multiple elected representatives.

party and the urgency of the proposed laws. Because they are organizations, they are also more suitable to increase awareness for certain social problems and thus to become popular. And because the power of the parties is capped by the limit of one representative per winning party, it is not problematic to use a voting system that is linearly affected by popularity.

7 LARGEST MAJORITY VOTING

There are currently voting systems that satisfy the requirements for electing people's representatives and party representatives. For people's representatives, a good option is range voting[27] (also known as score voting); this method should at least include four options: disapproval (-1), active neutral (0), approval ($+1$), and abstentions (equivalent to passive neutral). In range voting, the average vote is used to rank candidates. Furthermore, only candidates with an average greater than 0 should be elected, because an average below 0 indicates that more voters are against this candidate. When electing party representatives, approval voting can be used. This is an asymmetric voting system in which you are "for," or "not for" (against or indifferent toward) a candidate.[28] A fixed number of parties could be elected by selecting a fixed number of the highest-ranking parties, or a variable number of parties could be elected with a fixed threshold.[29] Although these methods are described for electing just one candidate, multiple candidates could also be elected with them. This is certainly

27 rangevoting.org

28 en.wikipedia.org/wiki/Approval_voting

29 The latter might be preferable because the former creates a zero-sum game.

necessary to create inclusive parties (see chapter 2), and it is also needed to sample the variation in majorities that elect people's representatives.

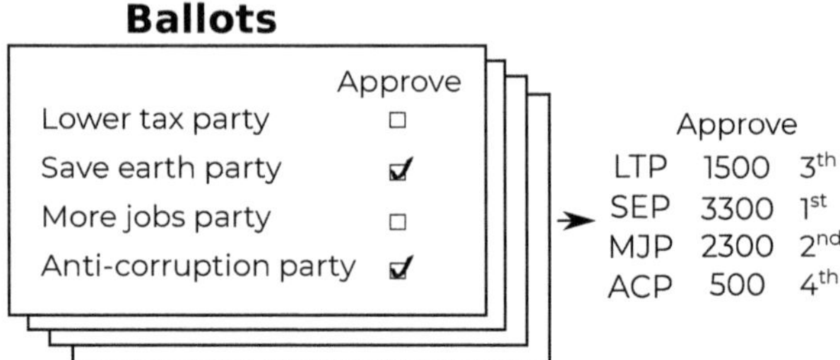

FIGURE 3.3: Outline of approval voting: an example of a ballot and the results of a hypothetical election. Candidate parties are ranked by the total number of approval votes. Parties can be elected based on their rank (e.g., the 50 highest-scoring parties) or a fixed threshold (e.g., above 10 percent of the electorate).

However, I find the averages from range voting to be nonintuitive. It is more clear to use the fraction of pro voters as a score—similar to the current majority voting system. For example, a normal majority means more than 50 percent of votes, and a supermajority is defined as more than a normal majority—60, 66.66, or even 75 percent of votes. This fraction of votes received can be used, much like the average in range voting, to rank candidates.[30] With this percentage, it is clear that candidates who receive less than 50 percent of votes should never be elected as people's representatives, even if they have the largest number of votes. The inclusion of an active neutral vote allows people to indicate that they do not support or reject a candidate. These neutral votes will not

30 This fraction is a transformation of any type of range voting method.

change a majority of votes into a minority, or vice versa, but they will decrease the size of the score, and therefore they can change the ranking of that candidate. In contrast, passive neutral (abstention) does not affect the size of a majority or minority. Furthermore, those who fail to reach the 50 percent threshold of votes should additionally not be eligible to participate in an immediate election; they should only be able to participate again in the next new election, or in case of early elections, after the normal term for which elections are held. This limitation will facilitate the removal of publicly distrusted politicians from the electoral pool. If reelection is necessary because too few candidates obtained more than 50 percent (e.g., the situation in Brazil, in which many members of Congress were being investigated for serious crimes[31]), the hope is that new, and therefore lesser-known, candidates will have a better chance.

31 www.latimes.com/world/mexico-americas/la-fg-brazil-impeach-20160328-story.html

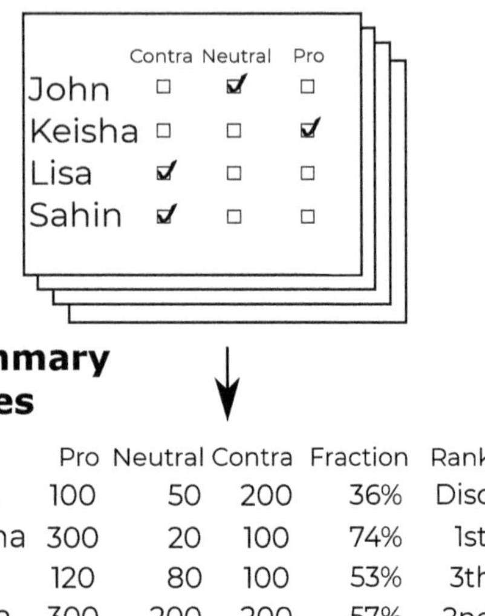

	Pro	Neutral	Contra	Fraction	Rank
John	100	50	200	36%	Disq
Keisha	300	20	100	74%	1st
Lisa	120	80	100	53%	3th
Sahin	300	200	200	57%	2nd

FIGURE 3.4: Outline of largest majority voting: an example of a ballot and the results of a hypothetical election. Candidates are ranked by the fraction of approval, but candidates with less than 50 percent (no majority) are disqualified (Disq.). For more info, see notes in appendix.

With this system, if a candidate is unknown, they could be elected by chance or because they have a strong, possibly small, motivated group of supporters that will vote positively. Fortunately, a soft quorum was developed for the range voting method.[32] This soft quorum easily enables the generation of an analogous version that is applicable for largest majority voting. In this version, a fixed number of neutral votes (an equal number of pro and contra votes) is added to each candidate's votes. This will push the frac-

32 rangevoting.org/BetterQuorum.html

tions of all candidates toward 50 percent. But candidates with few votes will be affected more than those with many votes. This method will not interfere with the disqualification of candidates because it cannot pull the fractions over the 50 percent threshold.

If people's representatives are elected by majorities, will all voters' opinions be represented by the people's representatives? Although the people's representatives should represent all people, they will likely hold the opinions of majorities.[33] Note that I explicitly use the plural form: majorities! This is possible because multiple, different majorities of voters will elect different people's representatives. The people's representatives being independent of each other will result in better representation of different majority opinions about different issues. Therefore, people's representatives will reflect the variation in majority opinions, while party representatives will reflect variation in all opinions. This system also provides a safeguard against the tyranny of the majority, in which one majority conspires to vote identically and suppresses the minority.

33 If the president of the United States speaks in another country, he should represents all US citizens, but his opinion will almost never reflect the opinions of all US citizens.

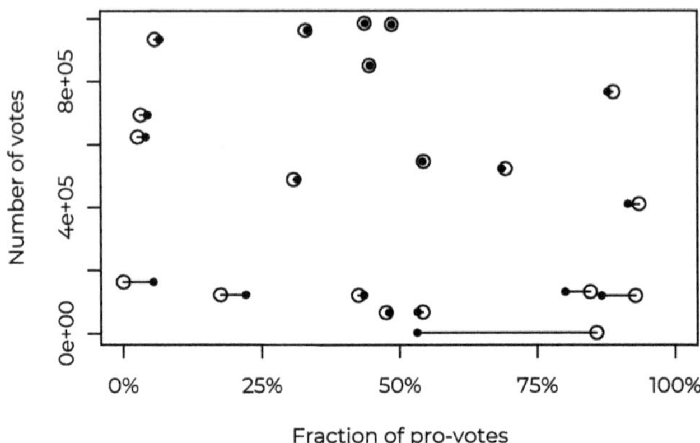

FIGURE 3.5: Scatter plot that illustrates how the fraction of approval is affected by the total number of votes for 20 random candidates, before and after the soft quorum rule is applied. Empty circles represent fractions before correction and full circles are fractions after correction. For more info, see notes in the appendix.

8 AD HOC PARTY REPRESENTATIVES

Separating party representatives from people's representatives will significantly increase the number of parties. Although we might have many parties, we only need a few parties to be represented by a single representative when we consider a specific law proposal. However, if the parties that can send a representative to parliament must always be selected during an election, we might not achieve the 10- to 100-fold increase of parties I stated as an objective in Chapter 1. In order to solve this, the separation of voting power and proposal power between the two types of representatives, together with the asymmetric voting method, would allow us to appoint ad hoc party representatives between elections. A petition could be used to appoint ad hoc party representatives.[34] This would facilitate new political input from different fractions in society without interfering with the balance of power (people's representatives), which can only be assessed during an election. Petitions are also a form of asymmetric voting because they do not distinguish between "against" and "unknown." However, attempting to create a petition as a symmetric voting method would fail because those that start a petition are biased to look for people that will support their petition. Hence, petitions are always asymmetric. Indeed, a petition can be seen as a form of approval voting in which the electorate can approve parties by giving a signature.

The use of ad hoc party representatives would increase the number of parties in two ways. First, it allows us to extend the time for supporting a party outside of elections. This eases the mental pressure on citizens, who might be overwhelmed by the immense number of parties in an election. It is also helpful for parties, because it reduces the participation threshold. Some parties may be organizations that are seldom politically active (e.g., a youth scouts organization). However, when a law is proposed (e.g., to prohibit nightly hikes), this organization should be allowed to politically react in parliament—much

34 It might be interesting to prohibit payment of those that collect signatures for the petition in order to prevent wealthy organizations from having an advantage over bottom-up movements.

like the long tail.[35] Many of these potentially politically active parties will only be sporadically active via an ad hoc representative. However, the combination of these parties can be a very important source of political power.

The ad hoc property is also important when no political organization yet represents a group interested in solving an emerging problem. This facilitates the simple creation of a new organization, without requiring a delay until the next election to act politically. The ad hoc representative would then have a mandate to represent an interest group within one lawmaking process.

9 THE LOBBYIST

The exclusive party system is only viable for a handful of political parties with established political power. Therefore, these parties have created a patronage position for which the representatives act as wardens of political power. Outsiders who seek to influence political decision-making are forced to convince the wardens (by lobbying) to support their cause, or they can start their own political party. The latter option is unlikely to work, as described in Chapter 2.

Because convincing politicians to support legislation is achieved outside of parliament, it is, by default, not public. This characteristic makes the lobbyist system poisonous. Whenever the lobbyist and politician do not feel that it is

35 The "long tail" refers to the distribution of the sales of goods that need almost no stock space (e.g., songs). It has been shown that the top songs do contribute for a large proportion of sales, but as the stocks of songs get larger and larger, the combined sales of all seldom-sold songs (the long tail) gets more and more important (Anderson, 2006).

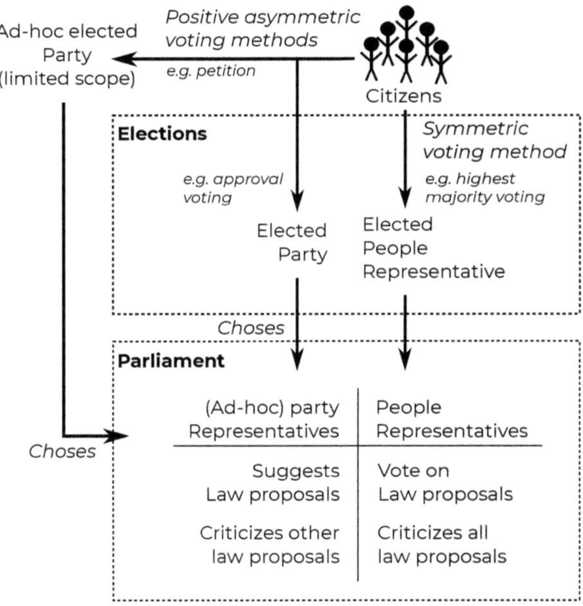

FIGURE 3.6: Scheme of a new representative system in which proposing and voting laws are separated. Different voting methods ensure that people's representatives will not benefit from polarization and that party representatives can be selected outside of elections.

in their interest to make their conversation public, they refrain from doing so. Reasons for private conversations can range from uncertainty about public opinion to arguments that directly oppose the public's interests, or even arguments that only benefit the private interests of the lobbyist or the representative. The latter can include promises of future jobs or direct corruption in the form of bribes. Even if the intentions of the lobbyist are good, there is no way to scrutinize arguments if they are not public. The success of parliament and other institutions such as the court of law are largely dependent on their public character.[36] The lobbyist system clearly undermines this, thereby undermining democracy.

Arguing that the interests of different groups balance each other is only valid if all interest groups operate under the same rules, which is not the case for bottom-up and top-down groups. Bottom-up interest groups are intrinsically more transparent; therefore, they cannot achieve the same results as a top-down lobbyist. This might explain the results of Gilens and Page, 2014: the independent influence of mass-based interest was not detectable, while business-oriented interest groups had a significant influence on lawmaking.

Because the proposals in this book lower the threshold to create a party and directly address parliament, people's representatives will no longer need to be influenced by lobbyists. Instead, assuming one has sufficient public support, an interest group (an inclusive party) can directly propose laws and policy in parliament. With this new system, it would be beneficial to implement laws that criminalize lobbying to influence people's representatives, much like laws

36 en.wikipedia.org/wiki/Open_justice

that prohibit people to influence a judge outside the court of law (violations of ex parte communication).

These changes to an inclusive system would convert the legal, but perverted, lobbying system into a public forum for discussions among interest groups (parties). This system is not intended to block all influence from top-down institutions. However, the requirements of popular support for political influence and the greater transparency of public debates in parliament will enable the population to be much more involved and to make those interest groups more responsible for their actions. Also, this system will counteract the advantages of multinational corporations over small businesses. This is because lobbying is relatively expensive, but small businesses might more easily receive popular support. As an example, few people will sympathize with their local division of a multinational food chain (neither the impersonally served customers nor the undervalued employees), but both clients and employees are more likely to sympathize with locally owned businesses. Innovations such as social networks, crowd-funding platforms, and petition websites have made it easier for small businesses and other grassroots organizations to gain support from large groups. The implementation of this new parliament, in which lobbyist are replaced by more transparent, single-issue parties, demonstrates how decentralizing politics will lead to the decentralization of the economy, as mentioned in Chapter 1.

10 ELECTORAL POWER OF PARTIES

Political parties exert power over candidates by determining who can be on the ballot. For most methods, like the first-past-the-post and proportional systems, the party decides who can be elected. In first-past-the-post, the person with the most votes is elected. This creates an incentive for each party to put only a few candidates on the ballot, because additional candidates might reduce the number of votes for each of the candidates. In a proportional system, the number of elected candidates depends on the number of votes for the party as a whole. This often results in a fierce clash between the most well-known candidates; other candidates are then often elected based on their position on the list, relying on the power of the party.

The system I present attempts to reduce the electoral power of parties down to control over a single seat, for which they can select a party representative who will not have the ability to vote on laws. In contrast, people's representatives will get onto ballots via public appreciation for their suitability and their historical associations with many different parties. This system will reduce the power almost completely that any party has over people's representatives.

CONCLUSIONS

The first aim of this book was to discuss decentralization of the political system. This is required in our complex world because our current democracy is fragile to external forces (e.g., economic elites, media, and foreign influences) and internal forces (e.g., polarization, political elites, populists, and coalitions). Furthermore, decentralization of our political system will also result in a decentralization of the economy. Many problems that we face are often incorrectly attributed to capitalism; in fact, problems result from an overly centralized economy, in which the most powerful companies have disproportionate power over our democracies.

Decentralization should be achieved through the transition of political parties from exclusive to inclusive. This will enable smaller parties, which can be combined and can cooperate, to better represent the needs of all citizens in our highly diverse society. The proposed system will provide greater freedom in political choices, greater participation, fewer large and unpredictable events (Black Swans), increased diversity of participants, and increased political innovation.

The proposed system will reduce polarization via three mechanisms. First, allowing citizens to participate and vote on multiple inclusive parties will decrease the bias that people have against "others". Second, a symmetric voting system for the election of people's representatives will limit the development of polarization. Third, although a positive asymmetric voting system for the election of parties is polarizing, this effect is strongly diminished by its qualitative character.

Because this system reduces polarization and prevents the alignment of representatives by party, it severely diminishes the risk of tyranny of the majority; in contrast, the tyranny of minorities is often a consequence of special institutions previously required to protect those minorities. Because the risk of tyranny of the majority is reduced, these special institutions will become obsolete. This framework is universally applicable, and it allows for more regional differences in party composition.

Because society is so complex, good predictions are impossible to make. Therefore, simple and well-defined changes should be preferred over broad and complex ones. In other words, piecemeal engineering should be favored over utopian engineering. By creating a political system that favors simple, one-issue parties over broad, "too big to fail" parties, piecemeal engineering can be realized in a concrete political framework. Although the system described in this book is new and therefore unproven, the use of simple and proven concepts (e.g., majority voting, court of law) favor the potential success of this political system.

Importantly, we should evaluate political systems based on their fragility to Black Swans. We should not forget one of the most harmful Black Swans of the 20th century: Adolf Hitler. The political system in which he came to power is hardly different from the systems we have today. Parties are still incentivized to become as large as possible, and citizens are still unable to confront the elite by voting against them. Much like today, the political spectrum was highly polarized. Since the political system has hardly changed at all, there is no reason we could not elect an equally extreme person with an even more devastating party apparatus supported by our technological innovations. Are we hoping for a miracle?

In contrast, we could decentralize our representative democracy, and a wave of bottom-up reforms could improve all domains of society. Perhaps even more importantly, democracy will become more viable for countries that are currently restricted in development by their self-serving political elite, therefore benefiting the entire world. While there is no promise of an utopian society, we can form a society that is well-equipped to face and overcome problems as they come.

PART II

APPENDIX

FAQ

Although this book focuses on the essentials required for a better-working representative democracy, mainly consisting of parties and parliaments, some questions beyond the scope of this book have been raised. My brief answers to some of these questions are included below.

- **What about digital democracy?** Although I am strongly convinced of the benefits that digitization can have on democracy, I am very suspicious of a democratic system that relies on digitization. The system would be too fragile; it could, for example, be targeted by cyber or nuclear warfare—especially when society is already in a vulnerable situation. For example, Tom Scott explains in the Youtube channel Computerphile why we should not do electronic voting.[37] There are many features concerning transparency, communication, and petitions that can be posted digitally, although digitization should not be required. In the economy, we see that the same "old" institutions, namely companies, have been able to adapt to digitization.

- **What about direct democracy?** Currently, I do not think that direct democracy is capable of completely replacing representative democracy because it is too inefficient. However, direct democracy is an excellent addition to representative democracy. Countries like Uruguay and Switzerland that use direct democratic

37 www.youtube.com/watch?v=w3_0x6oaDmI

methods are creating more anti-fragile societies. I think we can compare representative and direct democracy well with the two complementing mental systems described by Daniel Kahneman[38]: the first is fast and more unconscious, while the second is conscious and deliberate but much slower. Most of the time, the unconscious system will efficiently solve problems, but when needed, the conscious can override the unconscious system. Only when problems are very urgent should the conscious system be overridden by the unconscious one: e.g., fight or flight response by an organism or war for a state.

- **What about executive power?** This book describes changes to legislative power, without explicitly considering executive power. Since these powers should, in principle, be independent from each other, changing the internal workings of one should not affect the other. However, I do have some remarks about appointing the executive. In the instance of direct election of the executive (in presidential systems like the United States'), a symmetric voting system should be applied, similar to that proposed for electing the people's representatives. In systems where the legislature approves the executive (e.g., Belgium), that appointment should work as a legislative procedure: candidates can be presented by (ad hoc) party representatives, and then people's representatives will vote on which candidate should fill the executive role. This will result in individual appointments for all separate executive functions, rather than a single appointment of a complete cabinet. This was also proposed by Ostrogorski.[39]

38 Kahneman, 2011.
39 Ostrogorski, 1902, Vol II, p. 720.

- **Does the executive needs a supporting majority in parliament?** The previous question introduces my answer to this question: this is not a book on executive power. However, the executive should not need a supporting majority. For example, in the United States, the executive branch can function without a majority in Congress. Denmark also has a history of a well-functioning government that, since the late twentieth century, has only been led by a minority,[40] an arrangement that facilitates greater cooperation. Government should not be guaranteed a majority because a critical parliament works better for society—that is, a system of checks and balances; disagreement is key. Therefore, the direct control of both the executive and legislature by the same political party is detrimental for democracy.
- **What about party financing?** Controlling party financing in order to improve democracy is likely to fail because it does not address the causes; it only addresses the symptoms of an over-centralized political system. There are two different financing models: private and public (aka, state). Although both have benefits and disadvantages, in each case the disadvantages increase when political power is centralized. Consider the US political finance model, which emphasizes private financing. It has enabled private companies to hold too much power over policies. But a shift to state-financed parties would allow the two parties in the United States to further discriminate against smaller parties and opposition, especially if previous elections determined the funds allocation for subsequent elections. Regardless of the financing model, a centralized political system will

40 Green-Pedersen, 2001.

facilitate the worst outcomes because it is fragile. A more decentralized political system will prevent private interests from ruling via private financing, and it will be difficult, if not impossible, for few parties to use state financing models to suppress other parties.

- **What about lottocracy (also known as sortition)?**

  Depending on its implementation, lottocracy may or may not be compatible with the system presented. For example, the proposal of David van Reybrouck attempts to eliminate the use of political parties, making it incompatible with the proposed democratic system.[41] However, people's representatives from a parliament, as described in Chapter 3, could be chosen by lottery instead of via a symmetric voting system. My preference, however, is for the latter option. First, I do not think it is wrong in itself to have a people's representative with more experience serve multiple terms—especially when the symmetric voting system can remove incapable people's representatives. Having multiple terms by random chance is highly unlikely. Second, elections can also be considered to be a very costly, decentralized system—this makes them much harder to corrupt without notice. A lottocracy could be easily corrupted by those already in power because choosing a random person is a very simple process. Third, people become more political engaged when they are allowed to vote—one of the goals of democracy is more political engagement by all people.

41 Van Reybrouck, 2013.

- **Does your proposal, in which all political organizations become parties, complicate things?** No, because it only makes the complexity that already exists transparent. In fact, it reduces the complexity of the system by removing the wardens (exclusive parties) that shielded political civil society from directly interfering in the lawmaking process.

- **What about Arrow's impossibility theorem?** According to some, representative democracy would be impossible because Arrow's impossibility theorem proves that all voting systems are imperfect. These people are pointing to the voting of representatives, apparently forgetting that there seems to be no problem with voting for laws. Indeed, as I stated in Chapter 3, we should primarily focus on electing good representatives (A vs NOT A), not on electing "the best" representatives (A vs B vs C vs ...). Fortunately for us, when there are only two choices, Arrow's impossibility theorem does not hold.

NOTES
and additional ideas

These are some additional notes and ideas that are independent of the main goals of the book; they may still be useful to discuss and to combine with the proposed system.

1 LARGEST MAJORITY VOTING AND THE SOFT QUORUM RULE

On figure 3.4 and 3.5 of Chapter 3: The formula used for the largest majority voting is $Fraction = \frac{P+\frac{1}{2}N}{P+C+N}$, where P is the number of approvals (Pro), C is the number of disapprovals (Contra), and N is the number of active neutral votes.

The scatter plot was generated with twenty random hypothetical candidates. The soft quorum correction is applied by adding a fixed number of neutral votes (N_F), and hence the formula becomes $Fraction_{corrected} = \frac{P+\frac{1}{2}(N+N_F)}{P+C+N+N_F}$. In this case, N_F was 1 percent of the number of voters ($= 10^4$).

2 TRANSFORMATION OF RANGE VOTING INTO LARGEST MAJORITY VOTING

Any range voting method can be transformed into the largest majority voting method with the following assumptions:

1. Every person can cast one vote on each question.
2. The lowest and highest possible scores in the range voting method correspond with complete approval and complete disapproval of the given choice.
3. Any vote (V) in the range voting method can be described as a linear combination of complete approval (A) and complete disapproval (D):$V = aA + dD$, for which $0 \geq a, d \geq 1; a + d = 1$.

For example, consider a range of voting election choices: $-2, -1, 0, 1, 2$. The vote 0 can be transformed into $\frac{1}{2} \times \{-2\} + \frac{1}{2} \times \{2\}$, and the vote -1 can be transformed into $\frac{3}{4} \times -2$ and $\frac{1}{4} \times 2$.

We can see majority voting as a transformation of the range voting method. The largest majority voting method is then the range voting score of the linear combination of complete approval and disapproval. Therefore, the largest majority voting can be derived from any range voting method with minimum (S_{min}) and maximum (S_{max}) scores, rescaled by $s^T = \frac{s - S_{min}}{S_{max} - S_{min}}$. The disqualification threshold of 50 percent in majority voting is the mean score of the optional scores.

3 RANDOM CRITIC CONSTITUENCIES

People's representatives should defend the common good. However, if the group of citizens (or region) that selects and votes for representatives is smaller than the group of citizens (or region) they will represent, there is a reasonable chance that the voting result will be biased in favor of the voters. A potential solution to this challenge is to only work with ballots on which all candidates for the parliament are listed. For example, in Belgium, a federal list was proposed to allow Flemish, Brussels, and Walloon electors to vote on a combined list of Flemish, Brussels, and Walloon candidates. But this might result in a system that is not as scalable. Combining all candidates from different regions will either result in impractically long lists or will increase the threshold for a candidate to get onto a list.

An alternative solution would be to use randomized control constituencies. Suppose we have a list of candidates from a certain constituency. Then, the electors of that constituency vote on that list, together with electors from a randomly chosen constituency. Because this added group is random, the candidates will have to address people (and issues) outside of their constituency. If a candidate seeks election, they will have to address all electors because this random group could be anyone. Furthermore, because constituencies are randomly chosen to act as controls for the election of candidates, the importance of drawing constituencies will be diminished, reducing the influence of gerrymandering. For this method to work well, electoral sizes of the different constituencies should be similar.

4 FINDING AND VOTING ON THE MOST SUPPORTED LAWS

Let us assume that there are three parties (A, B, and C). Each party receives 33.3 percent of votes. In the current system, the parties only need more than 50 percent of the vote to pass a law, and political parties mostly control the members of parliament. This presents two problems. First, these parties will not investigate the law with the most popular support; instead, they will attempt to compromise with another party, or parties, to vote for the law that aligns with their interests. Second, the final law submitted to a vote is highly arbitrarily. It might be a compromise between party A & B, A & C, or B & C—all three laws can be very different—yet all are supported by a different majority. Most likely, the final law will not be a compromise between A, B, and C, because this would require extraordinary effort from all three parties, without necessarily forwarding their cause. An example can be seen in Figure 3.7.

Finally, compromises between competing interests do not guarantee that the compromise will actually be better for the general population. In the parliament described in Chapter 3, there is separation between party representatives (who propose laws) and people's representatives (who vote on laws). We could determine a procedure (algorithm) for parliament to determine which law has the most support, not merely sufficient support (+50 percent). For a political problem, each party could have a preferred solution. Instead of parliament considering one law proposal at a time, the people's representatives could vote on multiple competing proposals from different parties. As parties will support laws closest to their interests, the laws they

FIGURE 3.7: Positions of three parties located in a space of support by the people's representatives. Whenever two parties seek compromise between their points of view, they should look for a proposal on the lines connecting them—probably somewhere in the middle of those parties. However, these compromises might not have much support from the people's representatives or even the whole population.

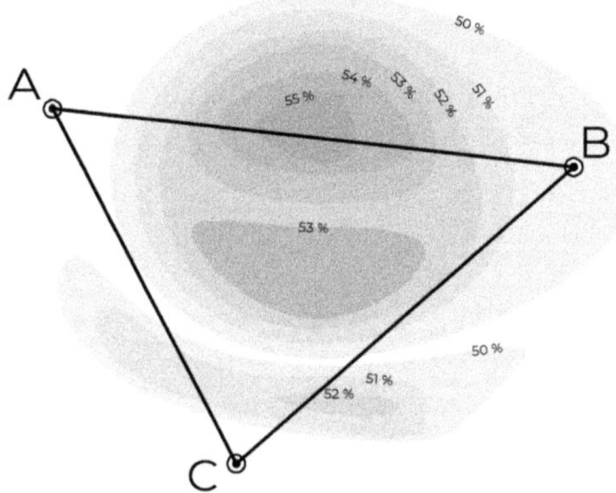

propose will be a compromise between what they like the most for themselves and that which they think will have the most support from the people's representatives. People's representatives can, for example, vote for the largest majority voting on the different proposals. Multiple cycles of new proposals will improve these proposals so that higher majorities can be obtained. Greater variation in political parties (more parties and bigger differences between parties) will facilitate a larger solution space for proposals, allowing society to direct the efforts of competing parties into searches for better laws.

FIGURE 3.8: Plots of two consecutive rounds of law proposals. Parties propose laws that are closest to their interests and also likely to pass. The encircled numbers are the law proposals that obtained the highest majority vote and won. (a) Point of view of parties who are unaware of the underlying approval space. Full dots are their proposals, and crosses are the proposals that they think are most likely to win. (b) Point of view of theoretically underlying approval space given by people's representatives.

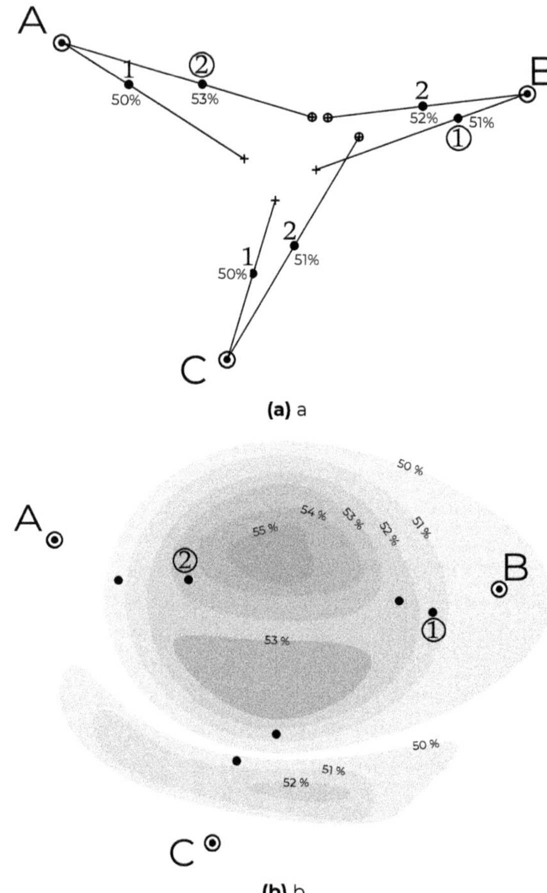

(a) a

(b) b

REFERENCES

Acemoglu, Daron and Robinson, James A. (2012). *Why Nations Fail: The Origins of Power, Prosperity and Poverty.* 1st. Crown.

Alcantud, José Carlos R. and Laruelle, Annick (2014). "Dis&approval voting: A characterization". *Social Choice and Welfare* 43.1.

Anderson, Chris (2006). *The long tail : why the future of business is selling less of more.* Hyperion.

Barker, R. and Howard-Johnston, X. (1975). "The Politics and Political Ideas of Moisei Ostrogorski". *Political Studies* 23.4.

Bonner, John T. (2004). "Perspective: the size-complexity rule." *Evolution; international journal of organic evolution* 58.9.

Burke, Edmund (1774). *Speech to the electors of Bristol.*

Del Giudice, Marco (2015). "Gender Differences in Personality and Social Behavior". Elsevier.

Derman, E. (2011). *Models Behaving Badly: Why Confusing Illusion with Reality Can Lead to Disaster, on Wall Street and in Life.* Free Press.

Eulau, Heinz et al. (1959). "The Role of the Representative: Some Empirical Observations on the Theory of Edmund Burke." *American Political Science Review* 53.03.

Gilens, Martin and Page, Benjamin I. (2014). "Testing theories of American politics: Elites, interest groups, and average citizens". *Perspectives on politics* 12.3.

Giles, Jim (2005). "Internet encyclopaedias go head to head". *Nature* 438.7070.

Green-Pedersen, Christoffer (2001). "Minority Governments and Party Politics: The Political and Institutional Background to the "Danish Miracle"". *Journal of Public Policy* 21.1.

Huyse, Luc (2014). *De democratie voorbij.*

Iyengar, Shanto and Westwood, Sean J. (2015). “Fear and Loathing across Party Lines: New Evidence on Group Polarization”. *American Journal of Political Science* 59.3.

Johnson, Eric J. and Goldstein, Daniel G. (2004). “Defaults and donation decisions.” *Transplantation* 78.12.

Johnson, Samuel and Zeckhauser, Richard (2014). “Status Quo Bias in Decision Making”. *Journal of Risk and Uncertainty* 1.1.

Kahneman, Daniel (2011). *Thinking , Fast and Slow.* Farrar, Straus and Giroux.

Katz, Richard S. and Crotty, William J. (2006). *Handbook of Party Politics.* SAGE Publications Ltd.

Michels, Robert (1911). *Political parties : a sociological study of the oligarchical tendencies of modern democracy.* Werner Klinkhardt.

Ohno, Susumu (1970). *Evolution by Gene Duplication.* Springer-Verlag.

Ostrogorski, Moisey Y. (1902). *Democracy And The Organization Of Political Parties, Vol II.* Macmillan and Company Limited. URL: https://archive.org/details/democracyandtheo033151mbp.

Ostrogorski, Moisey Y. and Lipset, Seymour M. (1982). *Democracy and the organization of political parties.* Transaction Books.

Popper, Karl R. (1945). *The Open Society and Its Enemies.* 1st Editio. Routledge.

— (1959). *The logic of scientific discovery.* Vol. 268. 3. Routledge.

Raymond, Eric (1999). “The cathedral and the bazaar”. *Knowledge, Technology & Policy* 12.3.

Sen, Amartya (1999). *Development as Freedom.* Oxford University Press.

Sherif, Muzafer et al. (1954). “The Robbers Cave experiment intergroup conflict and cooperation”.

Smith, Adam (1776). *The Wealth of Nations.* Vol. 2. 56. Strahan and Cadell.

Surowiecki, James (2004). *The Wisdom of Crowds*. Doubleday; Anchor.

Taleb, Nassim N. (2007). *The Black Swan: The Impact of the Highly Improbable*. Random House.

— (2012). *Antifragile: things that gain from disorder*. Random House.

— (2018). *Skin in the game : hidden asymmetries in daily life*. Random House.

Taleb, Nassim N. and Blyth, Mark (2011). *The Black Swan of Cairo*.

Unknown, Unknown (1902). *The Party System: Ostrogorski's Work on Democracy and Political Organisation (review)*. URL: http://query.nytimes.com/mem/archive-free/pdf?res=9502EED61E3DEE32A25754C2A9649D946397D6CF.

Van Biezen, Ingrid, Mair, Peter, and Poguntke, Thomas (2012). "Going, going,...gone? The decline of party membership in contemporary Europe". *European Journal of Political Research* 51.1.

Van Reybrouck, David (2013). *Tegen verkiezingen*. De Bezige Bij.

Voet, Donald, Voet, Judith G., and Pratt, Charlotte W. (2013). *Principles of Biochemistry*. John Wiley & Sons, Inc.

Vogels, Mieke (2014). *De rekening van de verzuiling*. Lannoo.

Werhane, Patricia H. (1989). "The Role of Self-Interest in Adam Smith's Wealth of Nations". *The Journal of Philosophy* 86.11.

Zhang, Jianzhi (2012). "Evolution by gene duplication: an update". *Trends in Ecology and Evolution* 18.6.

www.ingramcontent.com/pod-product-compliance
Ingram Content Group UK Ltd.
Pitfield, Milton Keynes, MK11 3LW, UK
UKHW021936190726
13853UKWH00004B/1474